TARGET SETTING AND GOAL ACHIEVEMENT

PROFESSIONAL
PAPERBACKS

TARGET SETTING AND GOAL ACHIEVEMENT

A PRACTICAL GUIDE FOR MANAGERS

SECOND EDITION

Richard Hale and Peter Whitlam

**KOGAN
PAGE**

LONDON, UK • NEW HAMPSHIRE, USA • NEW DELHI, INDIA

TO OLIVER AND WILLIAM

YOURS TO HAVE AND TO HOLD
BUT NOT TO COPY

First published in 1993 as *How to Introduce Target Setting*
This edition published 1995
Second edition published in 1998

Kogan Page Limited
120 Pentonville Road
London N1 9JN
UK

Kogan Page Limited
163 Central Avenue, Suite 4
Dover, NH 03820
USA

British Library Cataloguing in Publication Data
A CIP record for this book is available from the British Library.
ISBN 0 7494 2632 2

Typeset by Saxon Graphics Ltd, Derby
Printed and bound in Great Britain by Biddles Ltd, Guildford and Kings Lynn

Contents

Introduction   **1**

Part I THE CONTEXT OF TARGET SETTING

Chapter 1 Target Setting in Context   **7**
Targets and the Corporate Environment   7
Moving Training Back to the Workplace   9
Using Targets for Direction and Motivation   11
The Role of the Manager in Target Setting   12
. . . and Assessment   13

Chapter 2 The Emergence of Performance Management   **16**
The Purpose of Performance Appraisal   17
History and Trends   20
Examples of Performance Appraisal Schemes   23
Performance Management   27
Case Study: The Potential Pitfalls of Performance Appraisal   30
Higgins and York Case Study: An Alternative   33

Chapter 3 Integrating Target Setting with Existing Systems   **35**
Reward and Remuneration Systems   36
Competencies   38
Case Study: Achieving Balance in Target Setting   43
The Individual Problem   44
The Organizational Problem   45
Training and Development Programmes   45
Continuous Improvement   46
Case Study 1: Using 360 Degree Feedback at Coca-Cola Italia   51
Case Study 2: Reinforcing Company Values at Xilinx   55

Chapter 4 Preparing the Organization for Success through Target Setting   **58**

Time Constraints   59
Seniority   61
Administrative and Service Functions   63
Targets for Technical Roles   66
Not Everyone wants to be Promoted – Not Everyone will be
  Promoted   68
Target Setting in Team Environments   72

Part II THE PRACTICE OF TARGET SETTING

Chapter 5 Target Setting in Practice   **77**

What are Targets?   78
Quantitative Targets   79
Developmental Targets   80
Success Criteria   81
Top-down Support – Bottom-up Development   82
Reinforcing Organizational Messages   83
Using Targets to Breed Success   84
Example Targets   87

Chapter 6 Target Setting and Review   **91**

Preparation for Review when Targets are Set   92
Balancing Targets with Other Responsibilities   93
Encouraging Self-review and Continual Review   97
Timescales from Target Setting to Review   98

Chapter 7 The Interpersonal Skills of Target Setting and Review   **102**

Communication Skills   103
Listening   105
Questioning   106
Feedback   108
Confrontation   109
Perceptual Distortions   110

Part III TRAINING IN TARGET SETTING

Chapter 8 Training Managers and Employees to Set Targets   **115**

Model for an On-job Target Setting Workshop   117
Model for an Off-job Residential Training Course   118
Handling Questions During Training   121

Part IV GOAL ACHIEVEMENT

Chapter 9 Unlocking Human Potential   131
  A Model for Understanding Behaviour   132
  Characteristics of High Achievers   136

Chapter 10 Techniques of Goal Achievement   140
  Preparing for the One-off: Using Self-talk and Visualization   140
  Team Talk and Vision Building   143
  Using Self-assertion Statements   145
  Imprinting Self-assertion Statements   150
  Exercise: Managing Internal Change   151

References   155

Index   159

Introduction

Whether they are known as goals, targets or objectives, individuals and organizations are constantly seeking ways of achieving them. For individuals it is often a case of setting personal targets that will lead to personal and career development in a particular direction; for an organization, target setting is seen as a means of helping all employees to pull in the same direction with a view to gaining competitive advantage. Target setting provides the vehicle for the achievement of individual ambitions and dreams and for organizational competitiveness. All too often, however, the cry is heard that 'we cannot set targets because our jobs are different'.

In this book a number of clear guidelines are given on how to set targets in all functions of business and in all sectors. These guidelines are supported by many real examples of targets taken from organizations with which the authors have worked. For the manager, the advisor or the specialist in an organization, this is a practical guide on how to establish target setting and how to anticipate and work with the natural concerns that employees will have.

Part I considers major developments in how targets have been established and reviewed in organizations and in particular the emergence of the concept of performance management. It is explained that for target setting to be successfully implemented at an organizational level there needs to be astute recognition of cultural and historical factors. Included in this second edition are sections covering the concept of 360 degree feedback and target setting in a team-based environment, reflecting major developments in this area since the book was first published. Case studies taken from major international organizations and the consultancy work of the authors are included.

In Part II the practicality of target setting and review and the associated interpersonal skills are explored. Examples of different types of target are provided, drawing on real organizational experience. In establishing a target setting initiative the manager needs to design and deliver effective training; this might take several forms and some examples of training programmes are shown in Part III. Example course materials are included here.

In Part IV the authors discuss their extensive and original doctoral research into the subject of the achievement of human potential, which has led to the development of a range of techniques and models relating to the achievement of personal goals. These have been incorporated into the executive development programmes delivered by Peter Whitlam and Richard Hale, and have had positive practical results in terms of the achievement of human potential.

The origins of the research were in the sporting field where for some time anecdotal evidence has suggested that top sports people and athletes use a range of mental or psychological techniques combined with their physical training to help them attain their personal goals. Indeed, it is suggested that at the top level athletes are so closely matched physically that it is only by controlling their thought processes that they are able to gain competitive edge. The authors investigated the approaches taken by top executives in international organizations and found that they also used techniques incorporating visualization and imagery in order to help them achieve results. The incorporation of the term 'Goal Achievement' into the title of the book suggests that in order to increase the chances of personal development it is not only necessary to engage in good practice in terms of target setting, it is also important to ensure one's thinking is controlled and focused.

Overall, this edition of the book combines practical guidance and real life case studies with a sound theoretical and historical underpinning. Much of the work is based on consulting assignments of the authors who are indebted to their many clients including Coca-Cola, Lotus Computers, BP, Xilinx Semiconductor and Scottish Hydro-Electric.

Target Setting and Goal Achievement is a guide for managers who wish to use target setting to help others develop and improve their performance. Equally, it is relevant for managers or individuals wishing to focus on their own self development.

Those interested in discussing the subject with the authors are encouraged to contact them as follows:

Richard Hale and Dr Peter Whitlam, IMC Consulting, Broom Hill, 21 Cliff Drive, Cromer, Norfolk NR27 0AW, UK. Tel & Fax: 44 (0) 1263 515150 e-mail: hale@imc–c.com, whitlam@imc–c.com.

By the same authors

The Power of Personal Influence, Hale, R. and Whitlam, P., McGraw-Hill, 1995

Practical Problem Solving and Decision Making, Hale, R. and Whitlam, P., Kogan Page, 1997

Towards the Virtual Organisation, Hale, R. and Whitlam, P., McGraw-Hill, 1997

Powering up Performance Management, Hale, R. and Whitlam, P., Gower 1998

Part I

The Context of Target Setting

1

Target Setting in Context

SUMMARY

In this chapter we consider the context of target setting and why it is particularly appropriate as an approach in the light of important trends in organizations. In particular we consider the following factors and developments:

- pressures on the corporate environment mean that change is the norm;
- methods of training have developed significantly in recent years;
- training and development have moved back to the workplace;
- targets can provide direction and motivation for employees;
- targets can establish consistency across the organization;
- the key player in implementing target setting is the manager.

Managers should be aware of these overall developments and trends. Such awareness will provide breadth of thinking when considering how to implement target setting in the organization or department.

TARGETS AND THE CORPORATE ENVIRONMENT

In recent years the corporate environment has seen dramatic change and it is likely that the only constant for organizations in the future will, in fact, be change. This applies equally to the production and service environment and to the private and public sector.

Key trends have been:

- increased competition;
- shrinking markets;
- collaboration with competitors, customers and suppliers;

- higher customer expectations in terms of quality and service;
- a more fluid and demanding labour market;
- advancing technology and convergence of technologies;
- diminishing resources.

The pressures on all employees to do more with less have never been greater and the more astute managers are realizing that it is better to focus on doing the right things rather than simply 'doing things right'.

The following generic skills and abilities have now come to the fore. These skills are applicable in a range of situations rather than specific to any one job:

- teamworking;
- building relationships;
- interpersonal skills;
- persuasion and influence;
- knowing how to do things rather than just what to do;
- learning to learn;
- networking;
- being entrepreneurial;
- processing information;
- coping with change;
- problem solving and decision making;
- creativity.

Sometimes such skills are viewed as 'soft' or immeasurable. As a result, their development tends to be neglected and they are often avoided when it comes to setting targets. It is, however, just as possible to set real targets for these subjects as it is in the 'hard' or seemingly more tangible areas. Of course it is more difficult than setting, for instance, a production or sales target, but with a sound set of techniques and with the right spirit of implementation it is possible to set targets for *any* job. After all, if you do not know where you are going the chances are you will end up in the wrong place!

The key to surviving and potentially thriving in this dynamic corporate environment is for employees to understand what is expected of them and actually to have a say in determining the main targets for their job. They then need plenty of help and encouragement in working towards targets so that they are successfully achieved.

There needs to be open recognition from the organization of such success, even joint celebration within the workplace, followed by negotiation of new targets covering new issues. The whole process becomes forward looking – a way of helping the organization and the individual move successfully into the future. And if the focus is on success rather than failure the process also becomes self-perpetuating – success breeds success. So motivated by the successful achievement of personal targets and the recognition that this brings, employees will be hungry to agree the next set of targets for the future.

MOVING TRAINING BACK TO THE WORKPLACE

Traditionally we have trained people in job-specific skills such as sales, engineering, finance etc, and if they have shown the ability and inclination for management we may have offered management training. Management training in less enlightened organizations has invariably been made available after promotion rather than in preparation for the next move up; thus the major thrust of the training in such circumstances has been remedial: aiming to correct a deficiency or weakness rather than truly developmental. Unfortunately this is often how candidates also view the offer of training; it may be interpreted as an overt or implied criticism. How often have you heard staff boast that they have been selected for training? In organizations such as these it has been the sort of subject that has been whispered about almost apologetically.

Many organizations have survived with this approach to developing people largely because their structures are functional with little need to work across disciplines; each department working away in splendid isolation and only coming together through the coordinating efforts of the general manager. Of paramount importance in this scenario is gaining functional skills which will equip the person for life, if they are lucky.

Increasingly, however, organizations are realizing the importance of communication across functions and teamworking. In other words, business structures are regrouping with the main uniting factor being the customer or client rather than the department or the organization chart. Additionally the job-specific skills of yesterday and today will not necessarily be those of tomorrow; therefore it is becoming more important to enable employees to cope with changing demands and the need to be flexible, rather than to provide a set of specific skills which will last for life.

The other major change in the training world has been the diversification in the range of options now available as ways of training people. Historically there have been three types of training on offer with little variation available for those who did not really fit into one of the following categories:

- initial skills training – usually in the form of a time-serving apprenticeship for school leavers;
- professional training – usually for those who had progressed academically beyond secondary education; and
- off-job training courses – for those in industry unable to spend too long away from their place of work.

Increasingly, however, training has become recognized as something which should be continuous. The notion of skills has broadened and is constantly changing as technology develops; it is no longer possible to rely on initial or professional training given during the early part of an employee's career.

The ways of being trained are now many and varied. There is open or distance learning with multimedia methods and an emphasis on self-study; this might include workbooks, videotapes, computer-based training or interactive video. There is total flexibility regarding the time and place of study which offers the opportunity for a balance to be struck between the use of work time and the employee investing some of his or her own time. There is work-based coaching, secondment and mentoring. These all represent approaches to developing people which bring training much closer to the workplace.

There is much less emphasis on the classroom as the only environment for learning, and if we do decide to move away from the job for training, methods have shifted thankfully away from the 'chalk and talk' approach to more active 'hands-on' or experiential techniques of learning. The other major development in recent years is the advent of the competency movement. It is now possible to gain qualifications by demonstrating ability in the job situation; an excellent example of the working environment taking centre stage in the development process.

Furthermore, many companies have recognized the need to offer realistic and valuable support for the development of those at the most senior levels of the organization. Whereas in the past it may have been assumed that the more senior the person, the more knowledge and skill they possessed, it is now apparent that this is not necessarily the case. Increasingly, more forward thinking organizations are recognizing the need to provide personal support for the most senior of their executives in working towards the achievement of their job-related and personal goals. The authors have developed, with several of their clients, the concept of the 'executive coach', whereby a very focused needs analysis is conducted, followed by the development of a personal development plan; the executive coach provides expertise in terms of psychometric analysis, coaching, counselling, target setting and liaison with other key players interested in the executive's development. In many cases targets and associated development has focused on behavioural skills required to operate at a senior level.

Target setting then, if implemented professionally, also provides an opportunity to link development of skills and knowledge directly to the specific jobs of employees. By discussing and agreeing areas of priority for further attention it is possible to provide a framework for continuous improvement. If backed up by guidance and support both on and off the job, the individual will develop personally and be able to offer a higher level of contribution to the success of the business.

USING TARGETS FOR DIRECTION AND MOTIVATION

So target setting fits in with the movement of training and development away from the more academic and off-job situation towards the workplace and the needs of the individual. Targets can give direction to employees as well as a means of coping with the pressures of change. They can help the development of individual skills and can prove highly motivational: if they do relate to individual needs the process will have a high degree of validity and relevance in the eyes of the employee.

If pitched at the appropriate level for the individual they will provide 'stretch', which means that employees will realize that they do have capabilities beyond their current repertoire of skills and will be more motivated to achieve their full potential.

At the same time they can help at an organizational level to reinforce key messages about the culture and expected standards of work and behaviour. This does not mean producing an organization of automatons, because it is important to include targets which are specific to the development of the individual. Targets do, though, provide a means of establishing consistency in areas that have been identified as important to the values of the organization. This might, for instance, be to do with the image presented to customers, care for the environment, methods of communication, decision-making or formality and informality. The scope for reinforcing corporate values is enormous and targets can help pull a group of individuals together and face them in the same direction while drawing strength from individual abilities.

A few words of caution though. For any target setting initiative to succeed there needs to be top-level support and involvement. For anyone attempting to implement a target setting initiative one of the most difficult objections to deal with is 'I cannot set targets for my staff because my manager will not set targets for me'. Clearly there needs to be demonstrable involvement from the highest level down – and yes, you can set targets for directors and chief executives. Simply paying lip service to target setting is not enough; there needs to be an initial drive to set up a system that will involve professional and participative training in how to set targets followed by ongoing coaching and guidance.

All too often we see examples of organizations, with the best intentions, setting targets in such a way that they prove de-motivational or ineffective. The most common examples of these are where:

- targets are not positioned as a mainstream part of the job and the whole initiative is devalued
- targets are unrealistically high and set at impossible levels, thereby setting people up for failure
- targets relate only to organizational objectives, ignoring opportunities for personal development
- implementation of target setting is handled in an inequitable way by different managers, so setting the stage for claims of 'unfair treatment'.

THE ROLE OF THE MANAGER IN TARGET SETTING

The role of the manager in all this is vital. Professionalism and agile strategic thinking are required in identifying the links with – or distinctions from – existing initiatives such as performance appraisal and remuneration systems. Sensitivity to the culture and history of the organization is called for. Resilience is needed in dealing with the inevitable objections and fears.

For those who have seen organizational initiatives come and go before there may be a degree of cynicism: the 'We've seen it all before' syndrome. Such attitudes need to be anticipated and confronted with empathy. There will be some who fear that target setting heralds the advent of 'Big Brother' and that everything they do is being closely monitored and measured. These views must be addressed by creating a healthy climate for the implementation of target setting where everyone feels that they stand to gain personally in some way from the process. Then there are the spurious reasons for not being able to set targets 'here' because:

'we operate in a constantly changing environment',
'we have too many day-to-day pressures and interruptions',

'we are too technical',
'we are too creative – we work on inspiration',
'we are too senior for targets to be set at this level', or
'we provide an administrative service so we cannot work to targets'.

What all these objections signal is not the fact that it is impossible to set targets but that there is likely to be a lot of apprehension when the subject is first raised and that people have never been properly trained in setting targets.

Having laid the ground for the introduction of target setting and created the right spirit for cooperation and successful implementation, the subject of training should be addressed. Any training programme needs to deal with both the practical considerations of the target setting initiative (such as documentation and implementation strategy) and the development of target setting skills. Training should involve staff at all levels who are involved in target setting – either setting targets for others or having targets set for themselves. During training, delegates need to be able to practise drawing up targets using the ground rules and techniques they have learned.

Like most organizational initiatives it is not sufficient to deliver the training and just leave it to happen: with this approach it will wither and die. There is an instrumental role in giving ongoing support and guidance to employees at all levels. This will include further practical guidance for some and simply cajoling and lots of encouragement for others.

Once targets have become accepted as an integral part of management and a motivational tool it makes most sense to spread best practice throughout the organization.

. . . AND ASSESSMENT

Assessment is always one of the most contentious and emotional aspects of the target setting process. If, however, target setting is implemented effectively then it should be the most trouble-free aspect of all. This will mean ensuring that effective targets with built-in success criteria are agreed at the outset. Also it will be essential to ensure that there is open and ongoing dialogue regarding progress towards targets; in this way there are less likely to be surprises at the review stage. The review discussion will then focus on recognizing and summarizing what was achieved and why and offering support for continued development.

Human resource function	Senior management
• Overseeing the initiative	• Gaining agreement to introduce it
• Giving/obtaining specialist advice	• Selling the concept to senior management
• Administration	• Getting support to help sell it downwards
• Documentation	• Active involvement and participation
• Moderation of assessment	
• Linking to other HR systems	

New staff	All staff	Management	Consultants
• Induction	• Training	• Training	• Advising
• Appreciation	• Support	• Coaching	• Sharing best practice
• Setting initial targets		• Advice	• Confronting the 'accepted wisdom'
		• Help with assessment	

Figure 1.1 Target setting – the roles of key players

As can be seen from Figure 1.1 there are key roles for staff at various levels throughout the organization to ensure the success of any target setting initiative. At the senior level there should be support for selling the concept more widely. This will mean senior employees should 'practise what they preach' and work to targets themselves and set targets for their direct reports.

In a major strategic move towards a new channel marketing structure at Coca-Cola's Italia region, the authors introduced a 360 degree feedback exercise, where the top twenty managers were given structured feedback by their boss, colleagues and subordinates. From this exercise, personal development plans and targets were agreed. Significantly, and at his own request, the very first person to be assessed was the most senior executive.

There are also many parts the human resource department has to play, the most important being to ensure that target setting is integrated with other initiatives and systems. The obvious connection here is with performance appraisal but there may well be other links, for instance, to remuneration systems, training programmes and competencies.

Target setting presents tremendous opportunities for individuals and the organization and we will now look in more detail at how to overcome the difficulties and maximize the benefits.

ACTIVITY

What are the major economic, social and political pressures on your organization?

What are the major changes your organization is currently undergoing or is likely to see in the near future?

How is the organization responding to these pressures and changes in terms of preparing managers and employees to deal with them?

To what extent do employees work to targets?

How committed are those at the top of the organization to target-setting?

2

The Emergence of Performance Management

SUMMARY

In this chapter we consider target setting in the context of performance appraisal and the concept of 'performance management'. In particular we will focus on:

- the purpose of performance appraisal as a motivational tool and to provide valuable organizational information;
- developments in performance appraisal including the movement towards joint problem solving, focusing on results and the involvement of employees at all levels;
- the value of 360 degree feedback;
- important lessons from research on performance management.

It is important to be sensitive to whether one is operating in a 'performance management' organization and to identify the relationship between target setting and other performance-related strategies such as performance appraisal and performance-related pay.

This chapter includes case studies drawn from the experience of organizations the authors have worked with.

Rarely does a target setting initiative exist in isolation in an organization: the target setting approach and associated thinking is integrated with or at least linked to wider organizational systems.

The most usual and obvious link is with performance appraisal and the connection of target setting with performance appraisal is covered specifically in this chapter. In the next chapter we consider the links with other organizational initiatives and human resource systems, some of which will be deliberate and carefully contrived and others will be more tenuous but no less important and worthy of consideration.

Performance appraisal schemes take various forms depending on the history of appraisal in different organizations and on the style considered most appropriate. This will depend on such factors as sector, culture and job functions. There have been major developments in the field of performance appraisal in recent years and we will track these trends later in this chapter. First it is worth stepping back and asking the fundamental but often neglected question, 'What is the purpose of performance appraisal?'

THE PURPOSE OF PERFORMANCE APPRAISAL

Essentially effective performance appraisal schemes complement precisely the aims of target setting and thus it is most sensible to contextualize target setting within performance appraisal. As mentioned in Chapter 1 in relation to target setting, effective performance appraisal serves the purpose of enhancing the performance of both the organization and the individual. Realistically not all performance appraisal schemes actually achieve this; we will consider the reasons for this later on. In its worst form, for example, performance appraisal can have the effect of demotivating employees and generally lowering morale throughout the organization. Marginally better than schemes that have this effect are performance appraisal schemes which offer benefits and motivation to those who buy into the whole approach but neglect those who do not. Appropriately designed and carefully implemented performance appraisal schemes, however, offer massive potential at both the organizational and individual level.

Properly implemented performance appraisals should open up the opportunity for a healthy two-way discussion between manager and subordinate of performance over a recent period, and make plans for improving performance and developing the individual in the future. This forward looking focus is where target setting plays a major part and a key trend in recent years has been the evolution of this active and dynamic aspect of performance appraisal as opposed to the historic type of scheme which dwelt mainly on the past and static analysis of previous performance. The benefits of the forward focused approach are potentially more motivational. Peters and Waterman (1982) have developed our thinking on the subject of motivation through their research into successful organizations. In *In Search of Excellence* they identified the following basic needs which employees have in organizations and which excellent companies recognize:

- people's need for meaning;
- people's need for some control;
- people's need for positive reinforcement – to believe they are winners.

It was also explained that:

- Actions and behaviours shape attitudes and beliefs, meaning that a powerful way to influence employees is for managers to act in the way they would expect their employees to act.

As shown in Figure 2.1 there is clearly the possibility of satisfying all these needs through effective discussion of performance and planning.

Peters and Waterman factors	How performance appraisal can satisfy these needs
Need for meaning	Clear linking of individual jobs with the objectives of the organization
Need for control	Joint discussion between subordinate and manager regarding future job priorities and targets
Need for positive reinforcement	Provision of effective feedback from manager to subordinate
Actions shape attitudes and beliefs	Performance appraisal as the starting point for deciding future action which entails senior-level commitment to help the individual develop

Figure 2.1 Performance appraisal as a tool for motivation

By motivating individuals through effective performance appraisal and target setting, the ensuing enthusiasm is likely to have an infectious and synergystic influence on others; this multiplier effect will lead to benefits at sectional, departmental and ultimately organizational level.

You may be thinking that this is fine for those who are successful in the performance appraisal interview, but for the employee who is on the receiving end of a poor appraisal the effect is more likely to be one of demotivation rather than inspiration. In the case of unprofessionally implemented performance appraisal the effects could indeed include demotivation and feelings of low self-esteem, disgruntlement, unfair treatment, victimization and weakness. This does not mean that the less easy issues to discuss, such as areas for improvement or development, should be avoided in order for performance appraisal to motivate. If dealt with skilfully by the appraiser these issues can be discussed objectively and in a positive way, with the emphasis on guidance regarding future action and support that can be made available to help the individual hone existing skills and develop in the new areas. It is quite possible for the employee to leave the performance appraisal interview highly motivated by the fact that those niggling worries about possible weaknesses or areas of vulnerability have at last been discussed openly and that there is an offer of future support.

By discussing both strengths and weaknesses of individuals through the performance appraisal interview it is possible for managers and professional trainers to audit continually and systematically the knowledge and skill resources available in a manager's domain. The benefits of this quality of information are many and can help with, for instance, work planning, succession planning and generally improving the likelihood of being able to anticipate future problems and priorities, rather than being pushed into a fire-fighting mode of crisis management.

Finally, one of the key aims of many successful performance appraisal schemes is systematically to identify training and development needs. In forward thinking organizations the concept of training does not simply mean an off-job training course for remedial purposes but could include many other options in terms of method of delivery and duration: a number of examples are provided in the checklist in Figure 2.2.

- On-job training
- Further and higher education programmes
- Mentoring
- Coaching
- Secondment
- Sabbatical
- Job rotation
- Self development
- Open learning
- Teach-ins and workshops
- Job enrichment

Figure 2.2 Performance appraisal and the identification of training needs – methods of training and development

Performance appraisal can serve many purposes, the most important being motivation of individuals, the maintenance of morale, the identification of strengths and weaknesses throughout the department, and the systematic identification of training needs. The principle underpinning all schemes, whatever their design, is to remove subjectivity which is more likely to exist in appraisal without a consistent system or approach. Having considered the overall aims of appraisal it is instructive to track the trends in the design of performance appraisal schemes and how these relate to the increasing emphasis on target setting.

HISTORY AND TRENDS

The last 40 years have seen many changes in the development of performance appraisal but the most significant changes have occurred only recently. This implies that there is no panacea for the ills of previous initiatives, but certainly these changes constitute major advances and certain common factors have emerged which distinguish successful schemes from those fraught with problems. The underlying theme has been the emergence of individual target setting linked to organizational goals and we will show how this principle links to many of the other recent developments.

From Traits to Results-based Assessment

From the mid-twentieth century there was a growth in systematic approaches to appraising performance. Until the mid-1980s the emphasis in most schemes was placed on making judgements about employees against broadly defined traits and behaviours such as:

Cooperation
Leadership
Teamwork
Initiative
Attendance and timekeeping
Diligence
Interest shown
Presentation and appearance.

Often the same traits were used throughout the whole organization and assessment was a case of making fairly broad judgements in terms of categories such as excellent, good, room for improvement and poor. In the 1960s this approach was refined into the more systematic 'management by objectives' approach which attempted to apply a much more rigid methodology to quantifying the assessment of performance. Eventually this advanced and more scientific approach to performance appraisal became in many cases self-defeating. One of the problems experienced with such schemes was that as the documentation became more complex and onerous for the appraiser, it took on more significance than the actual process of generating healthy dialogue regarding performance. As performance appraisal systems became more and more complex, in some cases the objective of the appraisee was to beat the system and negotiate the highest rating possible.

With the more forward focused appraisal schemes, assessment tends to relate to the achievement of results and outputs linked to targets which were negotiated at the previous performance appraisal interview. Then, of course, there is the negotiation of new targets to work towards in the future. The targets-based approach, in comparison to the traits-based approach, places the emphasis on the achievement of results which are relevant to the needs of the individuals and their departments rather than making broad judgements against supposedly generic traits. A word of caution here; many management-by-objectives schemes failed because of the absence of links with the overall aims of the business.

From Effort to Results Focus

The move towards results-based systems has meant that the method of assessment has moved from attempting to measure the effort provided by employees to measuring results. Examples of effort and results measurements are shown in Figure 2.3.

Logically, to assess the effectiveness in a particular job role it is essential to focus on results despite the natural tendency to consider some of the items shown under effort as more relevant. This is covered in greater detail in Chapter 5 in relation to the target setting process in practice. A key role here is to develop, among users of the appraisal system – both appraisers and appraisees – an awareness of the subtle difference between effort and results. There should be a process for continually checking and challenging the targets produced by line management as a means of developing effective target setting skills.

From Judgemental to Joint Problem Solving

Traditionally the process of appraisal entailed the manager completing relevant documentation, often under pressure from the personnel department, behind closed doors. The appraisal interview consisted of, at best, a

Effort	Results
Effort	Sound decisions
Concentration	Accuracy
Attendance/Punctuality	Quality of work
Efficiency	Effectiveness
Attitude	Results achieved through others
Interest in job	Application of knowledge
Confidence	Application of skills
Enthusiasm	Problems solved
Self organization	Innovations achieved
Image	Targets met
Drive	Financial performance

Figure 2.3 Effort and results measurements

run through of the judgements made with no room for input or discussion by the appraisee and some advice on 'how to do better next time'. In even more outmoded examples of performance appraisal the appraisee would not even see or discuss the judgements made with the appraiser and no discussion would take place on areas of success or how to improve.

In the case of one appraisal scheme – operated in the 1980s in a major UK financial institutional – employees would be given an over-all grading of 'exceptional', 'highly effective', 'less than effective' or 'unacceptable'. Their grading was shown on the front of the appraisal form and, needless to say, this caused all manner of difficulties. There were, for instance, examples of employees, moving from one work area, where the manager assessed most people as 'effective', to another area where their new manager used the 'less than effective' option frequently.

So, an individual's performance might be sustained at the same level but their overall rating would be reduced simply because they moved job. Equally, there was uncertainty as to what each of these categories actually meant. This resulted in many employees simply attending the appraisal meeting knowing they could not influence the discussion, seeing little to no value in it and coming out of it thoroughly demotivated. Furthermore, given the close relationship of this appraisal system with the pay review, staff saw the appraisal process as simply the mechanism for distributing the annual salary budget amongst the departments.

Increasingly, however, it has been accepted that the most appropriate positioning of performance appraisal should be as a mature discussion of performance with the emphasis on jointly identifying and solving problems relating to performance as well as summarizing, recognizing and even celebrating areas of success and achievement. In fact, the more effective managers will continually appraise employees and provide ongoing feedback and support, if only on a less formal basis, and then summarize more formally at the performance appraisal interview. With this approach there are no major surprises for the employee at the performance appraisal interview and the stress and emotional charge is reduced leaving the way clear for a frank and healthy two-way discussion.

From Managerial to All Jobs

As it has become increasingly accepted that performance can and indeed should be measured in any job role so the practice of performance appraisal has spread from being the preserve of management jobs to being accepted as a legitimate approach at all levels of the organization in all functions and across business sectors. In Chapter 4 we show specifically how target setting can be applied in all kinds of job role and at all levels.

So the key trends in performance appraisal have been a move away from overly general assessments against stated, but in effect arbitrary, criteria and away from the more sophisticated but overspecific mechanical merit-rating systems. The most beneficial systems focus on individual targets which can be realistically assessed through collaborative problem solving and supportive discussion. Below we critique a selection of performance appraisal systems drawn from organizations we have worked with. Locke and Latham (1990) present evidence that goal setting is a major characteristic of appraisals that are effective in bringing about behaviour change.

Progressive organizations have made clear the relationship between improving the performance of the individual and meeting organizational objectives. This is the key tenet behind the movement which has become known as performance management.

EXAMPLES OF PERFORMANCE APPRAISAL SCHEMES

The examples below are drawn from a number of organizational performance appraisal schemes; only selected parts of each scheme are given to highlight key issues. The four approaches show the range of types of appraisal and will help the reader to consider some ways of addressing the paperwork side of the system. It should be recognized that performance review is about significantly more than the system alone and, indeed, some organizations have pursued the route of 'paperless appraisal' in order to overcome the problem of over-emphasis on form-filling.

The Tick-box Approach

Assessment Criteria	Very good	Good	Satisfactory	Needs attention	Poor
Quality of work					
Speed of work					
Cooperation					
Leadership					
Teamwork					
Initiative					
Communications					
Flexibility					

This is a classic tick-box type of appraisal system, where a list of criteria is provided and the appraiser makes the assessment according to a fixed range of options. There are a number of potential problems associated with over-reliance on such an approach. First, if the system determines that the criteria (leadership, teamwork, etc) are common for every job in the organization, there are likely to be jobs in which some of these criteria are irrelevant, or in fact the actual job entails other key performance criteria that are not accounted for.

Many organizations have begun to define competencies that form the basis for appraisal and target setting for specific jobs rather than trying to work on the assumption that the criteria are exactly the same for every job. Of course there may be some common criteria that apply to large groups or even the whole of the organization; these are likely to relate to the core values of the organization, for example, 'initiative' or 'teamworking', and in this case it is helpful to apply such criteria across the board.

The other major difficulties encountered with the tick-box approach relate to the scoring criteria. What does 'very good' actually mean, and is 'very good' from one manager the same as 'very good' from the next? Consistency is a core issue. Similarly, some schemes lead to the individual's total performance being summed up in one word or phrase such as 'effective' or 'less than effective'. This often leads to controversy over consistency and interpretation.

The other main problem with tick-box forms is the phenomenon known as the 'central tendency', whereby the person completing the form will naturally tend towards the central option rather than making more effort to discriminate. In fact, when the form offers an even number of options to try to get around this, managers will often redesign the form to create another (central) box!

So there has been a move away from relying exclusively on tick-box appraisal and many schemes now combine a tick-box element with the opportunity for narrative input.

The Narrative-based Approach

Comments against performance	Training needs identified
Job knowledge	
Planning skills	
Relationships with others	
Standards	
Other (complete as appropriate)	
Training undertaken	
Training planned	
Career plans	
Performance against targets for previous period	
Objectives/targets for next six months	
Comments from appraisee	

Here a number of criteria have been identified which are considered important for any job in the organization and an assessment is made in narrative form regarding performance. It is important to ensure that the performance criteria defined are in fact relevant to all roles; this needs some thinking through at the design stage. The problem encountered when organizations simply import a scheme from elsewhere is that often inappropriate criteria are included and the system then lacks validity for the managers having to work with it. Notice in this example that there is also the opportunity for the local manager to identify 'other' criteria that are relevant at a local level.

With this sort of scheme it is necessary to ensure that managers completing the documentation are willing to make balanced comments that they can back up with examples. Problems are sometimes encountered where a manager shies away from making more critical comments in writing or even writes in 'code', disguising the real meaning. The issue here is about being able to justify one's comments and judgement and being willing to confront the individual regarding their performance.

In this example you will see that there is an opportunity to identify training and development needs and to identify targets for the coming period. This provides more balance than the sort of system that simply assesses without any formal opportunity to link in with individual personal development. Many schemes now incorporate a personal development plan or position it as an adjunct to performance review.

There is also an opportunity for the appraisee to comment, which is an important factor when seeking to emphasize the joint nature of the appraisal process.

The Upward Appraisal Approach

This form of appraisal, whereby the subordinate appraises the manager, has become popular in recent years and has been tried in many different organizations. In this example the key competencies relating to the manager's ability to manage others have been defined (only two are shown) and the subordinate makes a judgement regarding his or her performance. The subordinate will use this form to provide some feedback during the subordinate's and not the manager's appraisal.

There are many options here. One key issue with upward appraisal is whether the feedback is anonymous or not. In some schemes the individual completes the feedback form anonymously and the feedback is processed by the personnel department. The argument in favour of this approach is

You are asked to provide some feedback to your manager against the key competencies which we have defined as being important in a managerial role. This will help to structure the discussion that you will have with your manager at your appraisal.

Rate your manager's level of performance against each competence along the scale provided. Be prepared to provide examples from the period covered in order to support your comments.

Empowerment	Encourages decision-making at the lowest levels	Devolves some decision-making and provides support when required	Is cautious about making information and opportunities available	Takes most decisions him or herself without discussion with subordinates
Development of others	Actively encourages and supports on- and off-job development of subordinates	Provides development opportunities if pushed by individuals	Takes a 'laissez-faire' approach to the development of others	Is unsupportive of the develop-ment of others
etc				

that the subordinate is likely to be more honest if it is anonymous and more guarded if it is not. The argument against an anonymous approach is that it may discourage open two-way discussion and feedback.

PERFORMANCE MANAGEMENT

Performance management describes the approach many organizations are taking to link individual targets to those of the organization as a whole; rather than operating as a specific technique it is more of a philosophy which potentially incorporates methods such as performance appraisal and performance-related pay. In a study of performance management in the UK, the Institute of Personnel Management (now the Institute of Personnel and Development) found that just under 20 per cent of responding organizations claimed to operate performance management systems (IPM, 1992). There were some important findings from this study with implications for the success of target setting initiatives. These are summarized in Figure 2.4.

As the number of management techniques has grown, including, for example, appraisal, job evaluation and performance related pay, they have frequently been implemented in the same organization in a piecemeal or 'bolt-on' fashion. Performance management takes an holistic approach and integrates human resource and management systems with the aim of

---

- Performance management organizations were likely to express performance targets in terms of measurable outputs, accountabilities and training or learning targets.
- More success was likely in organizations stressing the importance of ensuring human resource development activities and relating these to the needs of the organization rather than those where the remuneration dimension dominated performance management
- The challenge for the personnel function is to facilitate the ownership of performance management by line management
- Organizations implementing performance management systems should consider extrinsic needs of employees such as reward packages and intrinsic needs in terms of personal growth
- Training and development can be important motivators particularly if linked to career development.

Figure 2.4 Findings from 'Performance management in the UK – an analysis of the issues' (IPM, 1992. Reproduced by permission of the publishers. The Institute of Personnel and Development, IPM House, 35 Camp Road, London SW19 4UX)

continuously improving organizational performance. Figure 2.5 shows the wide number of management techniques and initiatives which could potentially come under the umbrella of a performance management philosophy.

Clearly performance management describes an approach to integrating the management of the performance of the organization with that of the individuals within it. This might be considered, as shown in Figure 2.6, to consist of a number of key stages in the employment cycle, each of which offer an opportunity for measurement of performance.

At the recruitment stage there is a responsibility for the employer to endeavour to ensure that there is a good fit between the skills of the individual and the requirements of the job. Furthermore, the candidate will need sufficient information to ensure that he or she is well enough informed to make a sound decision to accept or decline if an offer is made. Having key information regarding the sort of targets to expect to be working towards is vital at this stage. So being able to discuss target areas in broad terms or even to give some examples of targets agreed for previous incumbents is beneficial for the employer and potential employee.

The next stage of the performance cycle is where the employee is provided with information regarding what is expected of him or her by the employer. This is where initial targets are established and for an employee joining from outside the organization it is critical in terms of direction and

- Mission statement
- Business planning
- Training planning
- Performance appraisal
- Culture change initiatives
- Competencies
- Performance-related pay
- Job evaluation
- Communications initiatives
- Continuous improvement programmes
- Quality circles
- Succession planning
- Target setting:
  individual/sectional/departmental

Figure 2.5 Management techniques and approaches relating to performance management.

morale to ensure this discussion takes place sooner rather than later. This stage is often neglected when the job holder moves across from another part of the same organization. The danger here is that the employee makes an internal transfer but there is no change made to the targets that were set in the previous job; this obviously makes the review stage extremely difficult.

The next stage of the performance management model suggests that the employer needs to provide the employee with the opportunity to perform, which is about maintaining motivation. The issue here with respect to target setting is to ensure that targets that are set include some mention of the responsibilities which the senior person will undertake in order to help the

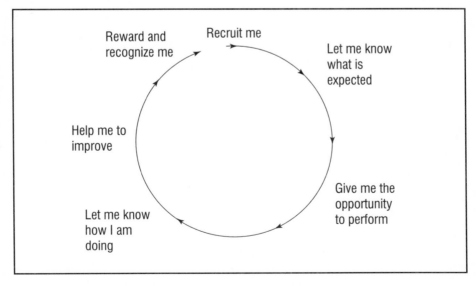

Figure 2.6 A model of performance management

employee through to achievement. This might include, for instance, making training available or the provision of ongoing guidance or coaching in support of the employee.

The fourth stage in the model says that there is a need to let the employee know how he or she is performing against the targets that have been set. This is for many organizations the formal performance review stage and is often covered by a formal appraisal system. Equally important to meet the needs of this stage, however, is the requirement for some form of continual, if informal, discussion about how the individual is doing. Linked to the review of performance is the need to provide assistance, either through a process of coaching or through counselling if there are specific problems to address, in order to help the individual to improve.

Finally, the model suggests that the individual can reasonably expect to be rewarded for effective performance. Clearly there are extrinsic rewards provided through the remuneration system. However, it is often factors such as recognition and the opportunity for further personal development that play a major role in an effective performance management system.

Target setting complements performance management and this may include targets which are set for individuals or working groups and which relate to individual or organizational objectives. Target setting offers the advantage of being able to define goals which relate to organizational aims at the same time as providing the flexibility of being able to tailor targets to the needs of individual employees.

CASE STUDY: THE POTENTIAL PITFALLS OF PERFORMANCE APPRAISAL

The Organization

Higgins and York are a well-established professional partnership tradition- ally renowned for their quantity surveying expertise but recently they have broadened into the field of estates management. They thrived in the period after World War II and their reputation was established largely as a result of the charisma and connections of the founding partners. In recent years they have found their market share eroded with the advent of a number of much younger, more commercial and dynamic organizations.

In response to this external pressure a recent merger has taken place with an historic competitor, due to the manoeuvring of some of the more pro- gressive senior partners. Some of the 'old school' professionals see this as the inevitable but unwanted change which signals the decline of the industry as they knew it. In fact, it marks the decline of the 'old boy network' as a way of doing business.

Senior-level teams from the other organization were tasked with introducing some of their good human resource practices into Higgins and York. This included the introduction of a new performance appraisal scheme. Until now Higgins and York have viewed such techniques as 'soft' and not really relevant to their sector.

The People

Ernest is an experienced, professionally qualified manager who has been with Higgins and York all his career and feels concerned by a number of the changes taking place in the industry. He also feels threatened by the recent merger of the organizations. In his day, he maintains, it would have been unthinkable to merge. Recently a redundancy campaign was completed and Ernest had hoped to secure voluntary redundancy associated with preserved pension rights. He was turned down and has now reconciled himself to the fact that he will need to 'keep his head down' and see how things work out for the future.

A year ago a recent graduate, Tom, was transferred into Ernest's department. Tom was recruited a few years ago as part of an initiative to bring new blood into the organization. Tom is partly qualified, bright and hungry for success and progression. He sees the merger as a great opportunity to make a name for himself with what will become a major player in the market. Ernest accepted Tom into his department under some duress while having to acknowledge his strength and enthusiasm.

The Appraisal

Tom was told on Friday by Ernest's secretary that his appraisal would take place on Monday morning. He was given no information about what would be expected of him or how the appraisal meeting would be structured but was hopeful that it would provide an opportunity to agree the areas where he had been successful in recent months since joining the department and possibly he might obtain support from the organization to attend a day-release programme so that he could complete his professional studies. He was a little concerned about some reports he had heard from colleagues in the department about their appraisals. Some said they were not really given a fair chance to input to the discussion so Tom decided to prepare some thoughts on paper in anticipation of the meeting. Generally he felt he had been doing well, certainly feedback from clients and other senior managers had borne this out. Although he had taken this commonsense approach he did worry over the weekend about how the meeting would go, conscious of the fact that this was a watershed in his career.

He had received very little feedback from Ernest during the year regarding his progress, but then he did not feel unique in this respect. It was generally accepted in the department that Ernest, while well respected for his experience, was not too comfortable talking to staff about their performance or anything rather more personal than simply the technical aspects of the job. It was also known that Ernest had managed to avoid the performance appraisal training which the organization had recently arranged, believing that there was not much they could teach him about management of people. It was also rumoured that he had had a less than easy time in his own appraisal with a number of his shortcomings being discussed for the first time in his career.

On Monday Tom had to see Ernest about a technical matter relating to a recent contract; the meeting was dragging on and Tom reminded Ernest about the booking he had for the appraisal meeting. Ernest said that they were too busy to cover it on the Monday and it could be 'knocked off' on the following day. Tom felt rather disappointed because, despite his worries, he had been anticipating the opportunity to discuss his performance with a hint of excitement.

On Tuesday the meeting lasted all of ten minutes! Tom was summoned to Ernest's office by his secretary and it was quite apparent that Ernest was nervous and keen to complete the meeting as soon as possible. He spent most of the time shuffling his papers and referring back to some guide notes. The conversation was very much one way and consisted of Ernest reading through a list of attributes Tom had never come across before and then reading out a grade. Grudgingly Tom was given a few good grades but was pulled up on a number of issues that he suspected were the same areas that Ernest himself had been criticized on. The main involvement that Tom had was to sign off the form at the end of the meeting: he did so, but with reservations.

Outcome

On reflection Tom was sorely disappointed about his appraisal; he confided in some of his friends about it, one of whom studied at college with him and now worked for a competitor. This friend had mentioned some time ago that there was a vacancy in his organization and 'wouldn't it be good if they could work together'. Originally he had dismissed the idea, particularly when he heard of the Higgins and York merger as he thought he would channel all his energies into developing a successful career with them. His friend mentioned that there was still a vacancy and suggested that Tom should come along for an informal discussion. Initially Tom declined but eventually he was persuaded that there would be nothing to lose in just making contact.

At the informal interview he was most impressed with the professionalism of the people and the environment, and to his surprise he was offered a position with the opportunity to complete his professional qualification through a sponsored open-learning programme. The salary offered was similar to that which he commanded at Higgins and York but the opportunities for development seemed much more attractive. He accepted the offer, gave in his notice with Higgins and York and left the organization just four weeks after his fateful performance appraisal interview.

Considering the case of Ernest and Tom at Higgins and York, list the various pitfalls which were encountered regarding performance appraisal. If you were responsible for the successful implementation of performance appraisal at Higgins and York what would you like to see handled differently? Having considered this case yourself you will find a number of suggested answers below.

HIGGINS AND YORK CASE STUDY – AN ALTERNATIVE

It should have been made obligatory for Tom to have had at least some form of performance appraisal training. This may have included coaching if he felt particularly threatened by the idea of a traditional off-job course.

Ernest should have spoken to Tom personally in advance of the meeting in order to agree the dates of the appraisal meeting and to discuss the format. This should not have been handled through the secretary.

The meeting date once fixed should have been adhered to. Cancelling the meeting only served to devalue its importance in the eyes of Tom. In this case it seems that Monday morning was not a good time of the week to arrange such a meeting.

During the meeting there was clearly a problem with paperwork constraining the flow of conversation. The discussion should have been balanced approximately 70/30 in Tom's favour rather than Ernest as the appraiser dominating the discussion.

It was also hinted that Ernest may have simply been passing on the issues discussed at his own performance appraisal interview to Tom. Clearly the focus should have been on Tom and his performance.

The tick-box system was not known to Tom. It should have been, and the style of the interview was very much judgemental rather than one of joint problem solving. In addition the good grades which Tom was awarded were given grudgingly rather than Ernest taking the opportunity to celebrate and recognize areas of success.

Tom was required to sign off the form at the end of the meeting rather than being given the opportunity to consider the content of the discussion. A more suitable approach would have been to give him time to think about the discussion and raise any queries or concerns at a later stage.

3

Integrating Target Setting with Existing Systems

SUMMARY

In this chapter we emphasize the importance of integrating target setting with other organizational and human resource initiatives and systems. The number of such initiatives and systems is potentially great but particular coverage is given here to some of the most important and topical:

- reward and remuneration systems;
- competencies;
- training and development programmes;
- total quality management.

It is important that in designing or implementing such initiatives to take an holistic approach, constantly seeking integration and links rather than 'bolting' target setting on to existing systems. Particular case studies are included relating to the work of the authors with Coca-Cola and Xilinx Semiconductor in introducing 360 degree feedback.

We have seen how target setting sits comfortably within the context of performance appraisal. It is worth considering how a target setting initiative might fit with other organizational development initiatives that have emerged in recent years. The danger of attempting to implement target setting without considering how it relates to other human resource initiatives is that it will founder; the accusation could be that it is 'just another scheme dreamt up by the personnel department' or that it involves 'more paperwork and administration; why can't we just get on with the job?'. For those responsible for introducing target setting the role can be made much easier by anticipating answers to questions such as 'But how does target setting fit in with total quality management/senior management training pro-grammes/competencies?' etc. Consideration of these issues demands strategic thinking on the part of the managers involved. We will consider some of the most relevant strategic issues below.

REWARD AND REMUNERATION SYSTEMS

A perennial debate in the field of performance appraisal is about whether the results of the appraisal interview should be linked to the reward system. In other words, should a good performance appraisal interview mean a good pay review? Remuneration systems differ widely across organizations but with the growth of performance management and increasing competition it has become generally accepted that, while specific methods of remuneration may differ, the overall logic of rewarding good performance is likely to encourage good practice. Many organizations in the private sector and increasingly in the public sector have created an atmosphere of meritocracy. The corollary of this is that there should be some connection between the process of assessing per-formance, ie performance appraisal or the measurement of the achievement of targets, and the system for rewarding performance.

In principle this sounds very sensible, however, there are a number of dif-ficulties associated with this approach. First, if employees being assessed are aware that there will be a direct and immediate link to a salary review they are quite likely to attempt to seek maximum personal gain. In extreme cases this can mean a tactical approach on the part of an employee. Tactics could include overemphasizing successes and strengths, playing down weaknesses and approaching the review of targets as a negotiation rather than as a joint problem-solving discussion. This hardly creates the environ-ment for the healthy two-way process referred to in the previous chapter.

To ignore the subject of rewards, however, can be equally destructive. There has been much debate and research into the motivational effects of pay and the summary of Charles Handy (1981) in his book *Understanding Organizations* makes some apposite comments. First, the tendency of money to motivate will vary for different individuals and it should be con-sidered as potentially the means of satisfying a number of human needs. This will include, for example, physiological needs such as shelter or food, or status needs such as being able to purchase the latest model car or a larger house. Second, money tends to be used as the basis for comparison with others. It is considered in relation to the rewards offered to those about whom the individual has a concept of his or her relative self-worth. This is likely to be a source of satisfaction or dissatisfaction. Relativity is often considered more important than the actual level of pay. Finally, a key motivator is often the fact that the individual has the ability to control the level of his or her income. This suggests that standard increments or across-the-board percentages are likely to be less motivational than, for example, rewards related to the achievement of individual targets.

At the time he wrote them, Handy's comments on performance-related pay may have been correct: 'Only entrepreneurs and insurance salesmen, among executives, experience money tied to particular pieces of effort. They are known to be particularly motivated by money'. There has, however, been a great spread in the practice of rewarding performance through payment systems and it is quite normal now to find performance-related pay schemes in white-collar and blue-collar, professional, service, product, private and public sector environments.

Given that it will not be uncommon for senior management, human resource or training specialists to introduce target setting in an organization where there is some form of performance-related pay, we should consider the practicalities of how to make appropriate connections between the achievement of targets and rewards. A key factor here is timing. If the pay award is to be made immediately after the review of performance against targets then clearly the review process will be emotionally charged and the risk of being drawn into the tactical game described previously will be high. If the review of targets is conducted some months before the salary review the emphasis can be placed more realistically on the subject of the targets themselves, how well they have been achieved, and the identification of targets for the future. Obviously when it comes to the actual salary review there will need to be some consideration of performance since the main target review to take into account any dramatic upturn or downturn in performance.

The other issue to consider is the extent to which the achievement of targets alone will affect the total remuneration package. Later in the book we emphasize that, while targets focus on key areas where successful performance will make an impact on the department and ultimately the organization, they do not necessarily cover the total job description. In other words, it would be quite possible for an individual to fail to meet certain requirements of the job not identified in targets and for this to have a serious effect on the assessment of performance. For example, timekeeping, manner in dealing with customers and attention to detail could be important qualities in a job: if standards are not maintained at a minimum level they could result in the tenability of the employees' position being brought into question. These qualities might not, however, form the basis of targets which would focus on overarching and forward looking subjects. When integrating a performance-related pay system and target setting it is important to consider which aspects of performance will have a direct impact on remuneration: what should be the balance in terms of targeted and non-targeted areas?

Similarly, salary reviews which include an element of performance-related pay often include other components not necessarily related to individual performance such as team performances a percentage linked to inflation, consideration of local market rates or industry-specific rates. Again it is important to distinguish clearly between these elements of the remuneration package and those linked to the achievements of targets.

It is worth noting that a study of performance management in the UK backed up previous research which failed to prove that there is a demonstrable link between performance-related payment systems and organizational performance (IPM, 1992). There is a danger then, in placing too much emphasis on remuneration at the expense of the 'softer' issues such as training and development.

COMPETENCIES

The 1980s saw the emergence in the UK of the 'competency movement' and throughout the 1990s our thinking and experience in this area have developed. There have been attempts to define the key areas of required performance in a job so that a recognized framework of competencies can be used for a number of applications in human resource management including, for example, recruitment and selection, training and development and succession planning. There have been many attempts to define what is actually meant by the term 'competence', the most appropriate and user friendly being 'The ability to apply knowledge and skill in the work situation and sustain performance over a period of time'. A key point here is the emphasis on the application of knowledge and skills. As training and education provision has evolved there has been a tendency for the development of knowledge and skills to take place in the off-job situation such as the classroom or management training centre with the inherent difficulties of transfer of learning to the workplace. The competency approach links the areas of skill and knowledge development to application, leaving open the way in which development might take place.

In the UK this thinking has led to the development of qualifications that can be achieved in the workplace. National Vocational Qualifications are achieved by working to standards that are expressed in the form of competencies. Such competencies have been defined on either an industry basis (for example, engineering, hairdressing, retail) or to cover occupations that cross industrial sectors (such as clerical skills and management). The intention has been to define generic competencies which are applicable in all organizations operating in the given industry or to all occupations in the relevant field. This has been a controversial exercise but there is no doubt that it has led to a quantum leap in our understanding of how the competency approach can be applied in practice. Figure 3.1 shows the key roles and their associated units of competency for the middle management role as defined by the industry lead body for management, the Management Charter Initiative (1991).

Some organizations have been quicker to draw on such work in the competency field than others. Unfortunately some have interpreted the publication of such competency lists as implying a straitjacket which does not fit well with the peculiarities of their own organization. Some, however, have realized that such systems need not be followed slavishly nor should they exclude the organization from enhancing the competency list with additional or supplementary competencies that are more relevant for them.

Key role	Units	
Manage operations	1	Maintain and improve service and product operations.
	2	Contribute to the implementation of change in services, products and systems.
Manage finance	3	Recommend, monitor and control the use of resources.
Manage people	4	Contribute to the recruitment and selection of personnel.
	5	Develop teams, individuals and self to enhance performance.
	6	Plan, allocate and evaluate work carried out by teams, individuals and self.
	7	Create, maintain and enhance effective working relationships.
Manage information	8	Seek, evaluate and organize information for action.
	9	Exchange information to solve problems and make decisions.

Figure 3.1 Key roles of management and their associated units of competence (Crown copyright)

Having defined the required areas of competency for different roles in an organization, the framework of competencies can be used in a number of ways to provide the 'cement' which binds and strengthens many human resource initiatives. For instance, competencies can form the basis for selection criteria against specific positions. They can be highlighted in job descriptions, person specifications, interview plans and might form the basis of criteria used in selection testing. Equally they can define subject areas for training and development programmes and might form a useful reference point in discussing individual training and development needs. Competencies can also help to define the subject of individual targets. Logically, if competencies attempt to define the requirements for effective job performance and targets are supposed to give individuals clear objectives for self development and organizational impact, then the two subjects cannot possibly be considered in isolation in the same organization. Figure 3.2 identifies some of the connections between competencies designed for the industry or organization and the types of target which might be considered appropriate in order to help employees develop competence.

For target setting to be of value for individuals it is necessary to ensure that targets do not simply replicate the competency framework, but use it to help provide a basis for identifying targets of relevance to the employee.

At this stage it is appropriate to spend some time considering the issue of behavioural competencies. The subject of how to define competencies associated with human behaviour has provided a particular challenge for development specialists in recent years. Furthermore, it is fair to say that in many organizations the emphasis has been placed on defining competencies related to the task of a job rather than the behaviours required to carry it out. The danger here is that one spends an undue amount of effort focused on outputs rather than behavioural inputs.

Organizational competencies	Individual targets
Generic competencies – defined by industry or function	Technical/skill-based targets, eg team building, financial techniques.
Departmental/sectional competencies	Locally applicable targets, eg use of a particular computing system, building relationships with other departments.
Personal competencies	Personal development targets, eg interpersonal skills, self-management skills.

Figure 3.2 Linking individual targets to organizational competencies

To understand this important theme, reference to the model in Figure 3.3 will help. Here we see a model of job performance that suggests that any outputs or results are actually the consequence of specific behaviours. Events or circumstances provide the opportunity for behaviours to be displayed and for results to be achieved. The common tendency in managing performance is to emphasize outputs. This in itself is not a bad thing because clearly results are important in any role; however, there are dangers of over emphasizing the importance of outputs at the expense of looking at the behavioural inputs that are required. Examples of job outputs might include for instance:

- production levels
- sales made
- numbers recruited
- courses delivered
- accounts paid
- procedures written.

If targets focus exclusively on the achievement of task outputs there can be problems such as the employee not understanding how to go about achieving results, or, potentially even more damaging, there is the danger of achieving results against the target but causing more disruption in the process than is often realized. Consider the case study below, taken from a real example of a sales executive who was extremely successful achieving against his sales targets. However, as the case study reveals, he was a

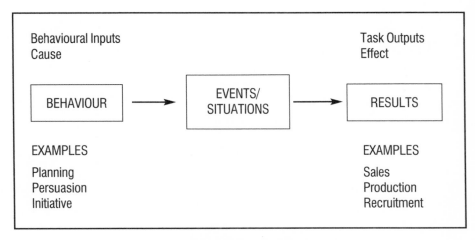

Figure 3.3 Understanding behavioural inputs

source of more problems in the way that he went about achieving results. The organization would have done better to take a more balanced approach by focusing on behavioural inputs as well as outputs.

If you were to analyse any task output and ask questions of a successful job holder such as 'How do you achieve the output?', 'What do you actually do?', 'Could you describe a recent situation and how you handled it?', you would eventually identify the key behavioural inputs required for success in the job.

In Figure 3.3 just three behaviours are shown by way of example. Human behaviour is made up of hundreds if not thousands of specific behaviours or competencies. Some examples of other organizationally related behavioural competencies are:

- attention to detail
- creativity*
- delegation
- development of subordinates
- flexibility*
- leadership
- listening
- numerical analysis
- oral communication
- problem analysis
- sensitivity
- teamwork
- tenacity*

Of course this is only a selective list of the many behavioural competencies that might be relevant in the workplace; you might think of many more. If it is possible to identify the behaviours that are critical in any particular job role, it should also be possible to define targets against these behaviours. By defining such targets and agreeing them with the job holder, there is more opportunity to focus on the behaviours or the 'how' rather than simply the 'what' has to be achieved.

Naturally, some behavioural competencies are more appropriate for development and therefore target setting than others. There is an argument that some behaviours are more innate than others. Consider for instance those behavioural competencies marked with an asterisk in the list above; how realistic is it to develop in others competencies such as creativity, flexibility or tenacity? Some behaviours tend to be more personality based and as such it may be more appropriate to seek evidence of such behaviours at the recruitment stage rather than trying to develop them in the job situation.

In order to explore this subject in more depth you might like to think about your own job role and consider the following questions.

What are main objectives of your job?	This will give you task outputs.
Taking each objective in turn, consider how you go about achieving them.	This will lead to identification of behavioural competencies.
Draw up a shortlist of six key behavioural competencies that you consider absolutely critical to success in your role.	You will need to differentiate between things that are 'nice to have' and those that are critical, in other words, without them you would surely fail.
Consider your current level of performance against these behavioural competencies.	You may be able to rank the competencies in terms of your ability.
Now consider how targets might be set against these behaviours.	See Chapter 5 for more guidance on how to set behavioural targets.

CASE STUDY: ACHIEVING BALANCE IN TARGET SETTING

The Organization

NetTech is a young and dynamic organization that operates in the field of cellular communications. One subsidiary of the business, NetTech Communications, designs and markets portable personal communications units, which are hand-held and provide telephone, fax and E-mail facilities. NetTech Communications was set up just six months ago and is headed by one of the original founders of NetTech, Max Johnson. It comprises a strong and aggressive sales team who target corporate business and a national network of sales branches selling to the public.

The Sales Executive

Ade Zimmerman is a sales executive in one of the biggest branches and was moved into this role when NetTech Communications was set up. He has been a key player in getting the organization off the ground, due primarily to his strong selling skills, his dynamic approach and his willingness to 'ask for the order'. Ade had joined the organization originally from a sales role in a financial services organization. He quickly impressed his managers by his ability to pick up the technical know-how required for his move to NetTech Communications.

THE INDIVIDUAL PROBLEM

Ade was delighted with his results for the last month. He had managed to exceed his sales targets by 20 per cent, which following the previous month's results put him on top of the sales team in not only his branch, but also the region. He knew what this meant: he was in line for the top sales incentive reward if he could just maintain his figures for the next two months. He had heard that the prize was likely to be an expenses-paid trip for two to Florida and he was already starting to taste the champagne in the Club Class seats on the flight to America.

Then suddenly he was summoned to the office of Max Johnson. He knew this must be to congratulate him – NetTech Communications were very good like that, always celebrating their successes. With a bounce in his stride he confidently rushed up to the top floor office suite to see Max.

The discussion that ensued came like a thunderbolt to Ade. It was very short and sharp and went along the lines of:

Max: Ade, if you do not shape up then you will be out of this organization. You have got six weeks in which to sort yourself out.

Ade: But what do you mean? There must be some confusion. You know my results have been outstanding.

Max: I know your sales figures have been good, Ade, but I think you know what I mean when I say you have something of an attitude problem.

Ade: No, I don't know what you mean. There is nothing wrong with my attitude. You can't lay this on me. I am the best sales executive you've got. You are going to need to justify this. I am going to seek legal advice.

Indeed, Ade did then go to seek advice from a friend he knew who worked as a human resource specialist. Gradually his friend managed to draw Ade out regarding what the problem might be. It transpired that there had been several incidents recently involving Ade and complaints from customers and from some of the sales team. There was one occasion when Ade was dealing with one of his own customers and another customer who was normally dealt with by a different member of the sales team interrupted their conversation because he was getting impatient with having to wait to be seen. Ade turned round and said 'What is wrong with you? You can just wait like everyone else. If you can't wait then clear off and come back later. Can't you see I'm busy?'

Similarly, there had been complaints from within the team that Ade was becoming increasingly aggressive with team members and was so competitive that he was withholding information that he felt would give him a competitive edge.

Thus, linked to Ade's clear strengths, which were his dynamic approach, his clear focus on achieving results and his competitive attitude, were a number of weaknesses. These weaknesses included a tendency to steamroller decisions, an aversion to consulting others and a style best described as one of 'fire-fighting'. But the organization's approach to target setting and rewards clearly did nothing to help Ade.

THE ORGANIZATIONAL PROBLEM

As far as the organization's system for motivating employees was concerned, there was a major emphasis on extrinsic rewards. In a sense this was not surprising as the entrepreneurs who had set up the business were very much motivated by seeing tangible results for their endeavours.

While the incentive scheme for sales executives worked well because there was a direct and immediate link between results and rewards, and indeed most of the sales team were primarily driven by a desire for visible rewards of financial value, there were some inherent drawbacks. There was no way of monitoring the behavioural competencies of the team; they were set targets against sales and nothing more. The system seemed to imply that making your sales was all that mattered and how you went about it was incidental. As far as Ade was concerned this meant that in achieving his targets he was actually causing more problems through his behaviour than benefit to the organization from the sales he was bringing in.

TRAINING AND DEVELOPMENT PROGRAMMES

Many organizations are introducing major culture change programmes in order to improve their competitive edge and survive in a dynamic business environment. Usually a major vehicle for such programmes is a series of training and development workshops or courses. Individual target setting can reinforce the messages behind culture change programmes by building core themes into targets. For example, if one of the key culture change themes is to increase proactivity then an individual target might focus on ways in which the employee could operate in a more proactive fashion at a local level. In this case the target could include, for example, subjects such as building external contacts, initiating new projects, or exercising more creativity.

Another major development in the field of training has been the tendency to coordinate different employee development interventions such as off-job courses, on-job development and educational training. The concept of the 'learning organization' suggests that the organization should continually transform itself by learning from everything it does and that in the future this is how competitive edge will be gained: through the ability and willingness of employees to constantly learn. But there are mixed messages here. On the one hand, any learning is good learning because it helps people learn to learn, which is an increasingly important skill in its own right. On the other hand, the provision of training in successful organizations is becoming better coordinated, themed and linked to strategic plans.

With either scenario target setting can provide a vital link between the identification of individual training needs and support for corporate training programmes. In the more forward thinking organizations training needs are identified in order to help employees achieve future targets as opposed to providing remedial training for those whose weaknesses are exposed after being promoted to their level of incompetence: the 'push' rather than 'pull' approach.

CONTINUOUS IMPROVEMENT

The 1980s and 90s saw a plethora of organizational improvement initiatives come and go. These have displayed themselves under different banners as organizations have sought for the secret which would give them a competitive edge; Total Quality Management, Continuous Improvement, Business Process Re-engineering are just a few of the most popular. Here we consider the relationship between some of the initiatives and target setting. Over all, it should be recognized that there is no easy answer, solution or initiative which guarantees success; more important is how the organization sets about continuously improving its strategies, structure and culture. There is arguably danger in adopting an 'initiative' approach – people are likely to see it as a proposed panacea, or at the other extreme, may take a cynical approach to what are seen as extremely important initiatives. Equally, there is a danger – which we have seen in some organizations – of suffering from 'initiative fatigue. In the following sections we look primarily at how target setting relates to Total Quality Management, but the key issues might be equally relevant if applied to similar initiatives with different titles.

Due in major part to the pioneering work of an American statistician, Dr W Edwards Deming, Japanese industry, which in the postwar period was notorious for producing poor quality products, became a major force in world markets. The turnaround was remarkable and the key was quality. Ironically, Deming had previously failed to convince his compatriots that focusing on quality was important and only by questioning and learning from the success of the Japanese did total quality management (TQM) concepts take root in the Western world. It is now difficult to find a sector which has not been touched by the quality revolution as organizations strive to meet the increasing expectations of customers, manage their supply chain more comfortably and differentiate themselves from the competition.

Total quality initiatives can utilize different techniques and may have a subtly different emphasis when implemented across organizations, but there are common underpinning principles. Some of the key messages behind TQM are listed in Figure 3.4.

TQM is essentially a philosophy rather than a technique and as such serves to facilitate consistent quality thinking throughout the whole

---

- Continuously satisfying the needs of the customer
- Redefinition of customer to include internal customers
- Getting it right first time, every time, on time
- Quality thinking runs throughout the whole organization and applies to all levels and functions
- Closer relationships with customers and suppliers
- Delegation of decision making and problem solving to the lowest level of the organizational structure
- Valuing the potential of all staff regardless of status
- Never walking past poor quality – everyone has a responsibility for quality
- Measurement of performance and establishing standards and targets
- Continuous improvement (the *kaisen* concept in Japan)
- High-profile training to implement total quality management which is followed through

Figure 3.4 Total quality management principles

organization at all levels and across all functions. In order to achieve this focusing of all employees in the same direction a range of effective techniques has evolved. Two issues that relate most obviously to target setting are developments in the field of problem solving and decision making and the concept of quality circles. We will consider these in turn and look at how target setting can contribute to their successful implementation.

Problem Solving and Decision Making

It has long been considered that one of the primary roles of management is to oversee the successful completion of tasks and to use financial and human resources to achieve this. Implied in this approach is the fact that the responsibility for defining problems and making decisions regarding their solution lies with management. Taking this approach to the extreme the autocratic style of management works on the basis that managers tell 'workers' what to do, reward those who do it and discipline those who do not. This is a crude summary but it highlights the contrast with the more successful and democratic approach espoused by TQM organizations which value the contribution that all employees have to make. The TQM approach recognizes that by helping all employees to identify organizational or operational problems and by equipping them with the skills to work towards their solution, the task of management is redefined. Rather than managers continually having to 'fire-fight' and being forced to operate in a reactive mode because they assume total responsibility for solving all problems, they are able to devolve some of this burden to others. Furthermore, there are likely to be less fires to fight under TQM because problems are proactively sought out and anticipated rather than simply reacted to. The priorities for managers in TQM organizations are to coach and encourage staff so that they develop problem-solving and decision-making abilities.

One of the major causes of failure of TQM implementation is that an initiative is launched with much enthusiasm and hype but initial training is not followed through with those who have to make it work. Problem-solving and decision-making skills develop over time with practice and employees need help in knowing when to apply specific approaches. This does not come simply with an initial training course; there is a need to provide continual follow-up support and this support becomes particularly powerful if it is built into individual targets. For example, at the target setting stage it might be possible to agree targets which reinforce TQM concepts by focusing on the following areas:

- developing problem-solving skills through off-job training;
- demonstrating problem-solving ability by identifying key areas to focus on and coordinating quality circles in working towards suggested solutions;
- demonstrating the successful application of problem-solving techniques, eg brainstorming, mind mapping, cost-benefit analysis, fishbone diagrams, force-field analysis;
- reducing the number of problems requiring crisis action through a proactive approach to anticipating problems.

Clearly these examples do not constitute targets per se, but could well form the basis for targets which would be agreed in detail following the guidance provided in Chapter 5.

Quality Circles

Those organizations which have introduced the quality circle concept most successfully have done so by translating the Japanese concept of work improvement groups into a language and style most appropriate to their existing culture rather than relying on direct mimicry. They have also integrated the quality circle approach into the wider context of TQM rather than relying on quality circles as a stand-alone initiative. In essence the quality circle approach is simple: small groups, typically comprising seven to ten employees, based on voluntary membership, come together to solve work-based problems which they themselves identify. This approach accepts that those actually doing the job are best placed to identify problems and propose solutions. Quality circles might comprise those at the lower end of the organization structure in shaping work methods and priorities.

As with TQM in general, one of the potential pitfalls with quality circles is that following the enthusiasm generated by the initial training programme there is little follow-up support for employees: the principle of delegation in fact results in abdication and there are no support structures to equip or encourage quality circle members to succeed.

As with problem solving and decision making, target setting provides the opportunity to give management support to quality circle members; quality circle concepts can be integrated into the everyday job. Subjects for individual targets could include:

- teambuilding;
- working in groups;
- presenting ideas to senior management;

- influencing upwards in the organization;
- meetings skills; and
- handling conflict.

Such skills, which are necessary for employees to be able to make a successful contribution to quality circles, are not developed by one-off training courses alone; it is essential to provide continual development opportunities and the facility to practise relevant skills and build confidence over time. Well-defined targets can help to ensure that quality circles do not collapse due to lack of support beyond the initial stage of formation.

Target setting might potentially impact upon a very large number of organizational or human resource initatives and policies. We have considered some of the most important and topical ones, but it is vital for those responsible for the implementation of target setting, consciously to work through the connections with those initiatives and policies operational in their own organization. Consideration will need to be given to the history and culture of the organization. In particular, when introducing target setting it is important to know whether management by objectives or performance appraisal schemes have been introduced before and how successfully. Anticipating these issues will help to determine which matters to emphasize when implementing target setting and delivering associated training. Success is more likely when there is an integrated approach to human resource management and activities are related to the needs of the organization. It is equally important both to focus on targets linked to developmental initiatives such as training and development and culture change and to make connections with the 'harder' issues such as remuneration and payment systems.

We conclude this chapter by presenting some case studies drawn from two organizations that the authors have worked with at strategic level. The first case study of Coca-Cola in Italy shows how the organization has redefined its structure, strategies and competencies in an effort to ensure its people are focused on, and reviewed against, those skills and behaviours that will be important in the future.

In the second case study we show how a world leading semi-conductor company has taken care to define key behaviours in order to ensure that its stated company values become real success criteria. Whilst both companies used the heading of 360 degree feedback to describe their initiative, what is really of significance here is how they have taken very much a strategic approach to ensuring that the measurement of personal performance is carried out against criteria which are considered most important to business success. This, we believe, represents a leading edge-approach and one which helps bridge the gap between individual and organizational target setting.

CASE STUDY 1: USING 360 DEGREE FEEDBACK AT COCA-COLA ITALIA

In 1997, following the commitment of the Italia region of Coca-Cola to a channel marketing structure, the authors worked with the organization to introduce a means of assessing and developing the management team against the key requirements of the future role. An overview of the key stages of the project is shown in Figure 3.5.

A structured process for defining the characteristics of success was adopted. It was realized early on that it was critical to understand how the role was changing and to ensure that managers were able to see how they measured up against this profile, rather than necessarily working from the basis of the job as it used to be in the old structure. Essentially, the channel marketing structure entailed focusing organizational structures and processes around what were described as 'home' channels, which included,

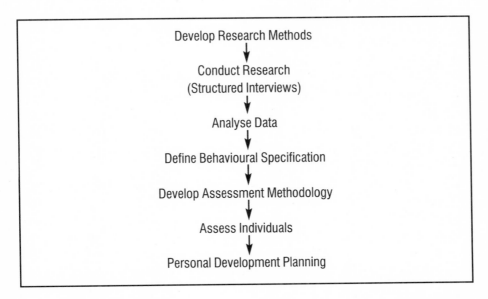

Figure 3.5 Overview of Key Stages in the Coca-Cola 360 Degree Feedback Project

for instance, retail outlets, hypermarkets and supermarkets, and 'away from home' which included places where people might drink the products whilst away from home.

Over fifty per cent of the management population was interviewed in depth in order to discuss how the role was changing and to identify the key requirements in terms of behaviours and personal skills. The following techniques were used during the interviews:

- Diary technique – individuals were asked to describe activities they had engaged in during an actual working day and the interviewers identified specific behaviours.
- Critical Incident Technique – in a similar way critical incidents from the recent past were described and key skills and behaviours were identified.
- Repertory Grid (Paired Comparisons) – interviewees were asked to compare and contrast a number of different managers they knew. In describing the differences and similarities it was possible again to see which were the key behaviours.

In addition to these interview techniques, managers were asked to complete a 'performance criteria questionnaire' that listed over fifty personal behaviours that are often seen in an organizational context, rating these behaviours in terms of importance in the changing role of the channel marketing manager of Coca-Cola. This enabled some valuable quantitative analysis that was combined with content analysis conducted on the data from the interview techniques described above.

A behavioural profile was defined and this detailed 32 behaviours that were grouped under the headings of Intellectual, Interpersonal and Individual and Leadership. Figure 3.6 below shows the behaviours against clusters. Intellectual behaviours were considered particularly important and comprised, for instance, of visioning, strategic thinking and business awareness. Interpersonal skills were becoming especially important in roles where managers were having to define and build new channels; here behaviours such as influencing, presenting and confronting were essential. Additionally, certain individual skills were found to be essential and they were categorized as such because there was an argument that they were more personality related and more difficult to teach; this included, for instance, initiative, the ability to make a difficult decision (which we termed 'emotional muscle') and commitment.

Once these behaviours had been agreed and defined, a questionnaire was developed which would enable assessment of individuals against the current and future requirements of the role and for the whole population; that is twenty managers. Assessment was conducted by themselves, their peers, their boss and subordinates.

This led to ratings by the four categories of self, boss, peers and subordinates and summary data was presented back to the individual managers. It was considered essential to maintain an appropriate level of confidentiality and so feedback was managed through a one-to-one discussion held between the managers and the consultants. This led to the growth of personal development plans, incorporating formal training, structured experience, and coaching opportunities. In some cases, discussion led on to the identification of future potential job roles and career moves.

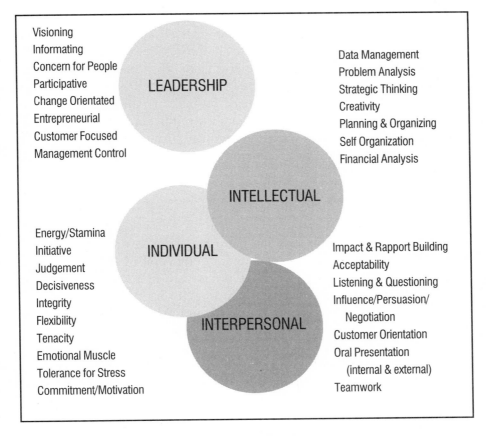

Figure 3.6 Coca-Cola Italia Behavioural Competencies shown by Cluster.

It can be seen in this case study that, due to the new business structure, there was a need for an objective reappraisal of job roles. Without this managers would have been assessed against the old, and therefore inappropriate characteristics of success. A number of interesting observations were made following the exercise. These are summarized below.

- Individual, or more personality related, behaviours present more of a problem for organizations: more often there is a need to recruit people into the organization who have previously demonstrated such behaviours as they are less easy to teach or train (how do you teach someone 'initiative' or 'commitment'?).
- In dynamic and changing environments there is a need to review the profile of the job, rather than work on old assumptions. In the case study organization it was apparent that some managers had strong skills in terms of the old role but had clear weaknesses or development needs when assessed against the new requirements.
- Senior management commitment to the process was essential in terms of establishing credibility and support from other levels. This was not simply a human resource initiative or a consultancy assignment, it was positioned as part of a wider strategic business imperative.
- Effort needs to be put into building up trust in the process. Whilst there was naturally some apprehension regarding assessment and how the data would be used, participants were encouraged to buy into the process through close involvement in the research, and through regular updates regarding the project.
- It was possible to validate the results of the exercise by comparing data produced through this exercise with that produced from other sources, such as performance reviews and more anecdotal data.
- Whilst most managers demonstrated a good level of self insight – in other words their self review was broadly in line with that of their manager – other patterns were seen. Some, for instance, clearly had an inflated view of their own performance and ability and this was seen where self-ratings were significantly higher than ratings of two or more other categories. Also there were some cases where individuals had a lower opinion of their own abilities than, say, their boss, peers or subordinates had; in these cases the issue of self confidence could be addressed.

CASE STUDY 2: REINFORCING COMPANY VALUES AT XILINX

Founded in 1984 and employing over 1,200 people world-wide, Xilinx is a world leading supplier of programmable logic and related development system software. Programmable logic has gained acceptance from a wide variety of applications and can be found in products ranging from network interface cards to phone switches, and from karaoke machines to ultra-sound equipment.

Xilinx is a 'fabless' semiconductor company, meaning that it does not operate its own wafer fabrication facilities: the company focuses on product design and market development. In the fast growing programmable logic market, a manufacturing strategy based on alliances is the optimal way Xilinx have found of operating. Xilinx is implementing a strategy of global expansion and considers Europe to be a crucial element of this expansion.

It is committed to developing a particular and well-defined company culture, building on the strengths which its people possessed right from the start. These are summarized in the company values statements which fall under the following headings:

- Customer Focused.
- Respect.
- Excellence.
- Accountability.
- Teamwork.
- Integrity.
- Very Open Communication.
- Enjoying Work.

Throughout 1997 and 1998 the authors have worked with Xilinx on the implementation of a 360 degree feedback exercise for all of the senior managers throughout Europe. In some respects the process adopted was similar to that described in the case of Coca-Cola above, however there were some distinctive features of the Xilinx approach.

Firstly, this was seen as a major opportunity to focus on the company values and, through a company-wide process, to ensure that they became much more than just laudable words on a page or 'motherhood statements'. Not that this was ever likely to be the case: in contrast to the approach taken by some less progressive organizations, rather than simply defining the values at the top and announcing them to the employees, the first draft was developed and then worked through with every member of the organization in a series of workshops. This led to a revised version of the values being published which incorporated the views of people at all levels. For example, it was felt that emphasis should be placed on encouraging members of the organizations to achieve a balance of interest in their lives, rather than being solely concerned with work.

The research regarding the definitions of successful performance was carried out, only in this case it was concerned with the role of a senior manager in Xilinx, whereas at Coca-Cola the emphasis was placed on the changing role of the marketeer in the new channel marketing structure. Then the key behaviours were integrated with the Xilinx values and grouped into appropriate clusters, resulting in a 120 statement, forced choice questionnaire with narrative comment sections for each cluster.

The senior managers were then assessed by their manager, all of their peers in the management team, all of their subordinates and in some cases by their internal customers. Feedback discussions were held with each manager on a confidential basis and, in conjunction with the independent consultant's, personal development plans were drawn up. Additionally, managers were encouraged to share with their own teams a summary of the feedback and to identify the personal goals and targets which they were committing to work towards in the future. Clearly managers were setting up an informal agreement with their own people regarding how they intended to behave in the future and for some this meant entering into open dialogue regarding their own strengths and weaknesses. This of course is not something that has been common in the traditional managerial environment, but fitted absolutely with the concept of 'very open communication' as stated in the company values.

Overall the process at Xilinx has meant that managers are assessed clearly against the preferred set of behaviours and that they cannot simply pay lip service to the company values. This has also led to some revelations regarding managers who may have created a strong impression on one party in the process, say their boss, but were not relating well to their own team. With direct quantitative comparison of perception by the categories of boss, subordinates and peers, such cases became obvious. Similarly, it was possible to see very clearly where managers had either an inflated self-perception compared to that of others, or indeed where they had a low self-image compared to how they were perceived by others.

ACTIVITY

Consider the human resource management and organizational initiatives which have been introduced in your organization:

- When were they introduced and how successfully?
- Which initiatives can be directly linked to target setting?
- Which initiatives are less directly linked to target setting?
- Try to anticipate the questions which might be raised by employees at different levels and in different functions of your organization about the connection between target setting and existing initiatives.

4

Preparing the Organization for Success through Target Setting

SUMMARY

In this chapter we consider some of the problems associated with establishing targets in specific types of job function or role. By anticipating these issues it is possible to deal with the reservations that will be encountered in different sectors of the organization. Specifically we will consider target setting for:

- those under time pressure;
- senior managers;
- administrative or service function staff;
- technical staff;
- valued employees who do not wish to progress through the organizational hierarchy; and
- those who may be ambitious but realistically are not going to progress further internally.
- team leaders and team members

By anticipating the difficulties of implementing target setting in their own organization, managers will be equipped to take a proactive approach to dealing with the various concerns of employees.

The success of any target setting initiative is dependent largely on how it is implemented; it is quite possible to have an elegantly designed system that fails due to problems associated with implementation. We will look in detail at the subject of training managers and employees in the skills of target setting and review in Part III, but it is also worth anticipating the many objections to target setting which occur as it is introduced in different functions and at all levels of the organization.

Often the individual will give various reasons as to why it is not practicable to set targets in their own job role or discipline. Sometimes there is simply lack of ability to see how targets can actually be set for a particular function. Often the root cause of this concern is the fact that the individual automatically associates targets with quantitative measures such as sales made, units produced, labour turnover or profit. Additionally, there is frequently an underlying fear that working to targets will mean that supervision will be tightened, discretion for the individual decreased and that the employee's every move will be scrutinized.

It is also usual for employees to see targets as linked to personal development and, by association, with career development and progression. For some this will be seen as an opportunity to gain recognition for their achievements. For others, however, it may be viewed as a threat or pressure, particularly for those who are less ambitious or lack confidence in their own ability to progress. One of the most common reasons initially given for not being able to set targets is lack of time. Target setting is seen as another burden to be imposed on the already busy manager.

By anticipating these objections and working through ways of recognizing and dealing with them the implementation of a target setting initiative is more likely to succeed.

TIME CONSTRAINTS

One common problem in implementing any human resource policy is that of encouraging managers to take ownership for what are considered to be initiatives that are in the best interest of the organization. The role of the human resource specialist has shifted from that of imposing and policing organizational change to one of facilitating change and enabling managers to develop 'best practice'. In organizations where the history of the human resource function has fitted with the old style, the introduction of target setting can easily be interpreted as 'just another scheme from personnel'. The predisposition of managers is likely to be dismissive and less likely to be cooperative where they feel that their time would be better spent pursuing activities relevant to their line function. This is much more likely to be the case where human resource systems carry with them excessive documentation and involve the completion of complex or extensive paper-work. The cry is bound to be 'Why don't they just leave me to get on with my job?'

An important point to consider when anticipating this argument is that for the manager under pressure through sheer workload and time con-straints, target setting can actually help improve the ability to manage time and relieve stress. For managers who are stressed as a result of under-dele-gation and have a tendency to take on too much work, target setting pro-vides a powerful lever for developing managerial styles that encourage the development of knowledge and skills among subordinates rather than feel-ing under pressure to hold personally all the expertise needed in the section or department. So the sorts of question which should be considered in anticipation of objections due to lack of time include:

- What are you currently doing which you could hand over to your staff by setting effective targets?
- What knowledge do you hold which could usefully be shared with your staff or could be developed by your staff with guidance through target setting?
- What skills do you hold which, if developed by your staff, will relieve you of pressure? (For example, chairing meetings, negotiating with sup-pliers and customers, controlling budgets or expenditure, recruitment, supervision of junior staff, report writing.)
- How could you coach your staff to take on some of your responsibili-ties?
- If you were being considered for promotion would a member of your staff be able to replace you? If not, you may be restricting your chances of promotion!

The potential benefits of working through these questions are twofold. First, there is the opportunity to develop the skills of subordinates through effective target setting, and then there is the opportunity to use this as a means of developing managers' skills in prioritization, delegation and developing people. Boyatsis (1982) found that skill in goal setting and planning was among the key determinants of a manager's success.

Furthermore, if there are targets being set at a managerial level and there are objections on the basis of time this may point to the need for the devel-opment of time-management skills. This need too can be reinforced through a target setting initiative. So the manager might work towards tar-gets such as:

Develop time management skills over the next six months so that you are able to allocate around 25 per cent of work time to developmental, future focused activity. To facilitate this you will

1 attend a short off-job time management training programme and implement time management techniques which have been learned;
2 share knowledge and skills with staff through an ongoing coaching initiative which will enable delegation of certain responsibilities.

Success will be measured by studying the amount of developmental compared with operational work being conducted in the working week without the need to work over and above normal working hours; to be reviewed at the end of a six-month period.

In a similar way, the issue of insufficient time may be related to stress management and this could be tackled by establishing, for example, the following target:

manage the demands of the job effectively by seeking balance between work and external activity, delegating downwards more and negotiating in a proactive manner which tasks are taken on from internal sources (managers and customers).

SENIORITY

One of the most difficult areas to establish targets of a behavioural or developmental nature is among senior management. The natural tendency is to suggest that targets at a senior level should only relate to easily measured factors such as sales, profit or production. Indeed, it may well be appropriate to measure success in these terms but it can be hazardous to place all the emphasis on such results at the expense of some of the target areas which have traditionally been considered less measurable and 'softer'. For example, it could be quite appropriate for a production manager to work towards a production target – say 3000 units per month. But if in achieving this target he or she manages to destroy relationships with suppliers, exhaust the production team and damage the reputation of the production department within the organization, the original target might have been better unachieved. While short-term and easily measured production targets might be met, long term the likelihood of continuing to meet them is greatly reduced. What is equally damaging is the fact that the production manager may have reduced the likelihood of a number of other people achieving their own targets.

There is a strong case for setting targets for the leaders of organizations, in that it also provides an opportunity to focus on the qualities of leadership which the organization wishes to espouse. We showed how, in the case of Coca-Cola (case study, chapter 3) the key behaviours associated with successful leadership were identified and used in order to assess performance and develop individuals. Targets relating to leadership skills defined in this way can ensure that the right style of leadership is encouraged. So, for instance, if 'care for people' and 'approachability' are seen as important, then targets can be set around these issues, especially if, for instance, a leader has a tendency to neglect such matters in his or her drive for task related results.

Another major problem experienced by managers moving into senior-level positions is a natural tendency to revert to carrying out the functions of their old job which they understand better and feel more comfortable with. Ultimately this will frustrate staff below who had seen their own promotion as an opportunity to develop new skills and experience but who are also pushed back into carrying out their old job. This is expressed well by Bob Garratt (1990) in his book *Creating a Learning Organization* and the key message is that we actually neglect managers once they reach the most senior positions in the organization in terms of training and development. The difficulty is often knowing what sort of training is really appropriate for general management and the natural inclination is simply to provide coverage of the same functional topics as those provided at lower levels of the organization but to dress them up as 'senior management programmes'. As there may be no formal training for the most senior managers it is often assumed that they have demonstrated sufficient potential to deserve their exalted positions and therefore do not need further training: all too often it is a case of 'sink or swim'.

Targets provide a unique opportunity to tackle this issue head on, without publicly making the newly appointed senior manager feel even more vulnerable and isolated. Targets could be agreed to cover such issues as:

- understanding the finance of the organization;
- understanding the market place/industry;
- the nature of the competition;
- learning about other functions;
- relating external trends and influences to the organization;
- developing the profile of the organization;
- strategic decision making;
- developing managers;

- improving internal communications;
- special technical projects; or
- organizational change.

Involving senior managers in the implementation of a target setting initiative is a vital ingredient for success. As soon as employees detect that there is not genuine commitment from the top the whole programme becomes devalued and will slide down the priority list for busy managers. A very powerful strategy is to involve senior management in the launch of the target setting initiative by, for example, asking them to publicize target setting and to support it overtly. Taking this one step further it is extremely effective if senior managers are involved in the actual implementation of the programme through, for example:

- input to parts of the training programme;
- running training workshops unaided;
- demonstrating that they are working to targets themselves; or
- requesting that targets are reported upwards once set.

Involving senior managers in running training workshops or in appearing for guest slots can prove to be a subtle means of developing the target setting skills and awareness of the senior managers without exposing them as delegates on training courses where they might feel inhibited through a sense of vulnerability. Every time managers contribute to a training workshop they will be buying into the process at the same time as making a clear statement to employees that senior management is committed to target setting.

ADMINISTRATIVE AND SERVICE FUNCTIONS

Frequently staff in administrative or service functions will feel that it is inappropriate if not impossible to set targets in their particular area of the business. Often this is due largely to the tendency to associate targets with functions having an obvious link with the success of business such as sales or production. Also for those in a support or staff function it may be felt that it is difficult to measure performance. Employees in a job role where they have little discretion over what they do, and where workload and the type of work is determined by outside forces, may feel that it is unfair to expect that targets can realistically be established. For example, for a cashier in a bank it might be considered that to set a target for generating leads for new business from contact with existing customers is unfair. This is because the cashier has no control over the number of customers using the bank. The number of customers could be influenced by factors such as the economy, the competition and the effectiveness of the sales and marketing department. Similarly, managers should be cautious in selecting subjects for targets which actually relate to standards that ought to be maintained as a normal part of the employee's job function. It is important to balance these standards-related criteria with targets that will help the individual and the organization move successfully into the future. Listed below are some examples of the sorts of subject which relate more to the maintenance of standards than individual development targets in service or administrative roles:

1 Maintain a level of absence through sickness of no more than five days per year.
2 Ensure work benches and machines are cleaned and tidied at the end of each day by commencing the clearing up procedure no sooner than ten minutes before the end of the shift.
3 Adhere to health and safety procedures and reduce the number of accidents in the workplace.
4 Maintain spending levels within the annual budget figures as agreed at the start of the financial year.
5 Halve the number of customer complaints over the next six- month period.
6 Respond to job applications within one week of receiving letters from applicants.

While each of these may be appropriate standards for different job roles they do not constitute developmental targets as such; they are standards which should be maintained and there is really no acceptable standard beyond:

1 No absence through sickness.
2 Total cleanliness of work areas.
3 No accidents.
4 No overspend.
5 No customer complaints.
6 No delay on response to applicants.

A number of organizations are successfully bringing about major quality improvements by focusing on such specific measures, identifying current performance and establishing improvements required. These measures are appropriate for groups of employees to work towards and by focusing on the achievement of incremental gains it is possible to contribute to the creation of a continuous improvement culture which can have major cost-saving effects for the organization. Such subjects should, however, be balanced with targets which have a more personal value for individuals who work towards them in terms of their own development.

While some targets of this nature might be appropriate for groups of employees where they carry out similar roles, it is just as possible to design targets which have a high personal value for those in service or administrative positions. Some organizations with groups of employees who carry out the same job role successfully identify some common objectives and then use individually tailored targets to help individuals develop depending on their own personal needs. This is a realistic way of acknowledging that generally similar job roles are being carried out and in many areas consistent standards are expected, but that each employee is unique and the organization recognizes they will have their own individual development needs. Some examples of individual targets for employees in administrative and service roles are shown in Figure 4.1. It can be seen in these two examples that the target specified serves two purposes:

1 It offers a means for the individual to perform more effectively and demonstrates that the organization is prepared to make resources available for this development.
2 It will clearly help the department and ultimately the organization in terms of two key service functions being carried out more effectively in the future.

Increasingly organizations are recognizing that there are internal customer/supplier relationships and that the key is to identify these links and focus effort on improving the service that a department or individual provides to the internal customer. This will ultimately lead to increased competitiveness externally. Quality consultants have estimated (DTI, 1991) that savings of up to 25 per cent of turnover can be made through this focus on quality service.

For the personnel assistant's job role identified in Figure 4.1 the possible customer/supplier relationships are shown in Figure 4.2. In target setting for the whole job it would be appropriate to define similar targets which focus on the needs of all categories of customer.

To help you understand the importance of service departments setting targets which relate to improved service to their customers you might like to attempt the following exercise:

Job role	Example of target
Personnel assistant	Develop and maintain effective use of the computerized personnel records system. Accurate records of employee details when checked against manually held information and production of error-free monthly reports. Successful retrieval of user friendly information for line management, demonstrated by good feedback from managers. Initial training on the system to be provided by short off-job training course given by the software supplier and then by ongoing coaching from the internal technical support department over the next six months. Progress to be monitored on an ongoing basis and reviewed after six months.
Receptionist	To develop an understanding of the structure of the organization's functions and different departments. To be able to recognize key managers at section level and above and to be able to recall the function of their department. This is to help familiarize the receptionist with the organization and the industry and will help when processing enquiries from visitors and callers. Progress to be monitored regularly and reviewed after three months. Methods will include obtaining literature relating to the structure and nature of the business, inclusion on circulation lists regarding personnel changes. It is expected that after three months the job holder would be able to escort a visitor or a new joiner on a tour of the offices, providing an introductory explanation of the functions of each section.

Figure 4.1 Examples of targets in administrative or service roles

TARGETS FOR TECHNICAL ROLES

In technical organizations or departments it is common to face objections to target setting on the grounds that 'It is impossible to set targets here because we are too technical'. True, it may be difficult to set targets due to the technical nature of a job and it may be problematic for the human resource specialist or trainer who may not have a technical background to understand all the details of specific job functions. This, however, is no reason for exempting technical departments from an organization-wide target setting initiative.

The key advice for those responsible for putting target setting into place in this sort of department is to work on two types of target: the technical target and the behavioural or developmental target. It may be quite possible to

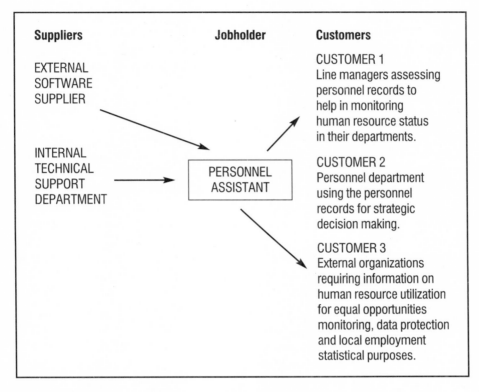

Figure 4.2 Customer/supplier relationships for the role of personnel assistant.

DEFINING TARGETS FOR SERVICE FUNCTIONS

Figure 4.1 provides a detailed target for the personnel assistant regarding the relationship with Customers 1 and 2 as shown in Figure 4.2; that is, line management and the personnel department. Using this as a model target, now attempt to devise targets as follows:

1. For the personnel assistant servicing Customer 3 – external organizations seeking information for equal opportunities monitoring, data protection and local employment statistical reporting purposes.
2. For the external software supplier providing a service, ie design, provision and maintenance of a software system for the personnel assistant.
3. For the internal technical support department providing a service to the personnel assistant to help develop understanding of the system and deal with technical problems.
4. Now you might like to identify the internal and external customer/supplier relationships for the receptionist identified in Figure 4.1 and design targets for the various suppliers in the relationship as you have done for the personnel assistant.

set technical targets which need to be agreed by a line manager who has an understanding of such issues and would be able to assess what would constitute a realistic, achievable and stretching technical target. Some examples of targets which have been set in technical organizations or departments are given in Figure 4.3.

These examples may help in considering the types of technical target which are appropriate to your organization. In dealing with technical departments, having persuaded managers of the benefits and feasibility of setting technical targets, it is important to stress the significance of not being over reliant on technical subjects for target content. It is equally possible to identify behavioural and developmental targets which can make an important impact on the department: it is natural, however, that technical managers will initially focus on the technicalities of the job role.

In terms of personal development some subjects for non-technical targets which could be introduced to technical departments are shown in Figure 4.4.

It can be seen that developmental targets might focus on issues such as the broadening of job roles and the development of interpersonal skills and supervisory management ability. For any employee in a technical role it is worth considering how specific technical skills can be balanced with such developmental objectives. Naturally the tendency of the technical experts will be to associate targets with the more technical achievements than the behavioural type of target. It is important to broaden the technologist's concept of what constitutes a legitimate target.

Interestingly, similar barriers to target setting will be encountered in creative environments where employees are likely to believe that it is not possible to establish targets where they work on 'inspiration', which is considered to be a natural phenomenon that might be stifled by the setting of targets. It is equally appropriate to focus on the developmental and behavioural types of target which have been shown in the context of technical roles. It is also possible to establish targets which in fact relate to the success of creative ideas.

NOT EVERYONE WANTS TO BE PROMOTED – NOT EVERYONE WILL BE PROMOTED

A common and legitimate cry against establishing targets in certain parts of the organization is that not all employees are ambitious and hungry for progression up through the corporate ranks. This point is worthy of specific consideration because it is true that the normal reaction to performance appraisal and target setting is that it is all geared to preparing employees for career progression. Clearly not all employees are aiming to progress in terms of working their way through the hierarchy and may feel that promotion is either unrealistic or undesirable. This is not to suggest that such employees are to be in any way undervalued. Often they form the lifeblood of the organization and with appropriate recognition will provide stability and continuity over a number of years.

It would be a mistake, however, to exclude such employees from the organization's target setting initiative; indeed, establishing targets and reviewing them provides an opportunity to recognize the achievements of those who often feel ignored in the event of organizational development and progress. With major changes affecting all sectors of business and the need to improve continuously it is possible to help employees to cope with changing practices and develop new skills by agreeing targets which could focus on, for example, new knowledge required and new skills to be developed. Very few jobs will remain exactly the same in terms of content over a long period of time and it is possible to broaden the experience of employees without necessarily expecting them to progress upwards. Including such employees in the target setting process may unleash unexpected potential, and the positive reinforcement which follows review of successfully achieved targets can maintain staff motivation at a higher level.

It is also important to recognize that some employees may reach a position where they are unable to progress upwards in the organization structure, yet are providing a valued contribution and, if suitably motivated, could continue to do so for some time. Often managers feel uncomfortable about developing such employees for fear of losing them to competitors. A broadminded approach to setting stretching targets in the current job role while recognizing that internal career progression opportunities are limited can in fact result in a useful contribution being made prior to an external career move, and is more likely to allow the employee to leave the organization on a high note.

Job	Example of a technical target
Network manager	Update and improve the network helpdesk operations procedures over the next six months focusing on the following: ● Attend helpdesk management training course and use skills developed to guide network operations staff. ● Produce a helpdesk user document which will be publicized and enable users to follow appropriate procedures. Success to be reviewed through feedback from users and review of the user document after a six-month period.
Engineering supervisor	Train shopfloor staff in the use of the new cutting machine so that they are able to set up, operate and carry out routine maintenance knowing when to draw on external help. Ensure staff are able to clean and close down machines without assistance within the next two months. This will be achieved by developing a written training programme and instruction manual.
Maintenance technician	Implement design modifications to the ZY product instrumentation which will satisfy the requirements of the test department within the next month. Design costs should remain within the budgetary constraints as agreed. Assistance where needed to be provided by the engineering service department and expertise available from the company training centre.
Buyer	Review the service provided by current suppliers of bought-in components in terms of quality, cost, delivery and reliability over the next six months. Make recommendations regarding the reduction of the number of suppliers to a preferred maximum of two per component type. Demonstrate an objective analysis by presenting statistical data on previous service over a stated time period and by making judgements of potential through a process of extrapolation and forecasting using information gleaned from structured interviews with suppliers.

Figure 4.3 Examples of technical targets

Job role	Example of developmental target
Production operative	Develop awareness of production techniques outside of current area of work so that you are able to explain to other employees the flow of production from kitting, through assembly to final testing. This will also help in preparation for movement on to other sections of the production department and will develop multi-skilled expertise. This will be achieved by temporary placement in other sections when workflow allows and by studying work instruction manuals from other sections. Time period for being able to supervise new staff to the department is three months.
Hardware engineer	Develop interpersonal skills with particular emphasis on presentation and influence in meetings. This will be achieved by attending the company presentations skills training course and structured reading combined with a gradual increase in involvement in team meetings and ongoing review of development through discussions with the engineering manager. Success will be measured by the ability to chair departmental meetings in the absence of the engineering manager and on a presentation on the work of the department to be given to other departments by the end of a nine-month period.
Project supervisor	Develop skills of supervision by delegating responsibility and coaching in technical aspects of project administration. This will be aided by the completion of a supervisory education programme combining open learning with development days over the coming year. Success will be measured by reviewing the improvement in skills of staff and their ability to cope in their jobs without close day-to-day supervision. Measures of the current ability of staff will be agreed now and targets for individual development established. The departmental manager will offer support by way of regular discussion with the project supervisor.

Figure 4.4 Examples of developmental targets for technical roles

TARGET SETTING IN TEAM ENVIRONMENTS

Increasingly, it has become recognized that team structures are likely to provide the normal unit of performance in oganizations (Katzenbach, 1993). Some writers such as Higgs and Rowland (1992) have even gone as far as to suggest that the emergence of team cultures is related to a societal shift in values from individualistic to collective and group values. Certainly their claim that team working is particularly important in situations of high uncertainty and maximum choice supported the findings of the authors as discussed in *Practical Problem Solving and Decision Making* (Hale and Whitlam, 1997). Furthermore, it is interesting to note how team values and behaviours featured high in the priorities of Coca-Cola and Xilinx (see case studies in Chapter 3).

So what are the key issues to consider if introducing target setting in a team environment? Overall, one should recognize the risk of placing so much emphasis on individual performance improvement that team related behaviours are neglected or even discouraged. Successful team players show a willingness to participate in the activities of a team even when the immediate task is of no direct personal interest and if targets are all focused on individually oriented subjects then one might expect to see individual team performance. So, in setting targets there should be a balance and this could be achieved by considering the characteristics of successful teams. We show the characteristics and the related target subjects which might be set for both team leaders and team members, in Figure 4.5 below.

ACTIVITY

Consider the various functions in your organization and attempt to anticipate the objections and barriers which will arise in response to a target setting initiative.

Against these objections and barriers attempt to outline some examples of targets which will prove to the doubters that target setting is not only possible but relevant and worthwhile. You may wish to refer back to some of the examples of targets given in this chapter to help trigger ideas.

Characteristics of successful teams	Targets for team leaders	Targets for Team members
Clearly defined goals and objectives.	Development and communication of a team vision.	Contributing to the development of the team vision. Working towards the achievement of team goals.
Understanding process for working together.	Establishing guidelines for communications (eg meetings, presentations) and standards for these.	Working to improve working methods
Appropriate leadership.	Providing right balance between task and individual focus as leader.	Leading the team through expertise in particular areas.
Opportunities for personal development.	Providing personal development for team members through training, coaching, counselling mentoring, etc.	Taking opportunities for personal development within team environment, eg coaching role-modelling, etc.
Strong inter-team relationships.	Building relationships and understanding with other teams, eg customers, suppliers, internal/external. Increasing the awareness of the team's objectives amongst other teams.	Building relationships outside of the team.

Figure 4.5 Characteristics and related target subjects which might be set for team leaders and team members

As well as the characteristics of successful teams as shown in the left hand column of Figure 4.5, it is worth noting the key behaviours shown by good team players. These are:

- openness
- trust and support
- assertive confrontation
- listening
- questioning
- sensitivity.

These behaviours might also form the basis for establishing effective targets for team leaders or members.

Part II

The Practice of Target Setting

5

Target Setting in Practice

SUMMARY

In this chapter we look at the practicalities of target setting. The following ground rules for effective target setting are established:

- focus on expected outputs;
- ensure a balance between quantitative and developmental targets;
- invest time in agreeing success criteria – it pays off at assessment;
- pitch targets so they are achievable but stretching;
- demonstrate management support for the process through action;
- involve employees in deciding their own target areas;
- use targets to help manage change and establish organizational culture.

Having tracked the trends towards target setting and the importance of 'selling' the whole concept into the organization we now need to look at the practicalities of how to set targets for individual employees. As previously stated there is no job or department where it is impossible to set targets, but the target setting process raises particular problems for different functions and job roles. It is critical that the good practices explained in this chapter are developed and spread throughout the organization.

It may help if you consider how you might apply the guidance given in this chapter to setting targets in your own job. Despite the particular problems of setting targets in different functions, eg sales, finance, production and personnel, there are a number of ground rules which will help when setting targets and ultimately will ensure that individuals contribute effectively to the success of the organization.

WHAT ARE TARGETS?

Targets are often known by other names such as objectives and goals but really these terms all describe the same thing. Targets explain what should be achieved at the end of an activity – a point to be hit or a desired result. The emphasis in this definition is important because the focus is on output rather than input or effort. Of course a particular target may be very demanding in terms of effort required to achieve it but the emphasis in the output statement is on the fact that it is achieved rather than how it was achieved. The guidance on how to achieve the target is discussed and agreed once the target has been described in terms of an output statement.

Figure 5.1 gives examples of output statements compared with input statements. These output statements alone are not comprehensive targets but would form part of a series of sentences which would make up a target. It is, however, important to understand the key principle of output statements first.

With the example shown of the secretarial input statement, doubling the amount of time spent on filing does not state the standard to be achieved or what level of efficiency is to be expected. The output statement, however, establishes a means of checking whether or not a target is actually achieved.

In the example of the sales input statement it would be possible to hit the target number of sales visits through increased effort but the effectiveness of such visits is not specified. With the sales output statement it might be possible by 'working smarter' rather than 'working harder' to achieve the sales target with fewer customer visits.

One of the first ground rules in target setting, then, is to include output statements. This does not mean simply attaching a figure to the target; we

Job role	Input statements	Output statements
Secretarial	Double the amount of time spent on filing.	Ensure all documents are correctly filed within 24 hours of receipt.
Sales	Conduct a minimum of four sales visits per day to customers over the next six months.	Increase sales of product x by 20 per cent over the next six months and increase market share by by 2 per cent.

Figure 5.1 Input and output statements

need to strike a conscious balance between what can be termed 'quantitative' and 'developmental' targets. Also it is equally important when setting quantitative targets to provide guidance on how they will be achieved.

QUANTITATIVE TARGETS

Take some time to consider examples of targets for job roles in your own organization. It is quite likely you initially thought of numerical targets such as:

- improve sales by 20 per cent;
- decrease errors by 70 per cent;
- achieve an efficiency ratio of 95 per cent on production machines;
- halve the number of customer complaints;
- produce 3000 units in the next month;
- recruit 30 graduate trainees by September;
- reduce the level of unauthorized absence to no more than six days per person in the rolling year;
- bring down labour turnover to under 6 per cent.

When realistically set these numerical targets are useful and they could apply at various levels: organizational, departmental or individual. If set for one person this type of target is geared towards the individual contributing to the wider aims of the business. Certainly if it is possible to build a realistic figure into such a target this will help both manager and subordinate share the same understanding of what is to be achieved. This will make assessment much easier at a later stage and ensure that there are no awkward discussions about what was originally agreed in terms of the degree of difficulty or standards. There are, however, dangers in relying too heavily on purely quantitative targets.

First, it is important when expressing a target in quantitative terms to provide some guidance on how the individual might achieve the numerical aspect of the target. If the figure relates to a departmental or organizational goal the target should be broken down to provide more specific guidance as in Figure 5.2. Here the detailed guidance is given on how the cost savings should be achieved. This will help provide focus for the employee and some concrete issues to concentrate on.

Second, when setting targets for a member of staff it is vital to strike a balance between targets which focus on the departmental or organizational goals and targets which are specifically intended to develop the individual.

Function	Overall numerical target	More detailed guidance
Marketing	To save the department over £200,000 over the next financial year.	Focus on effective buying of print materials and art work and negotiate discounts with quality external suppliers as well as making effective use of the internal print department.

Figure 5.2 Building on numerical targets

Obviously achieving the cost-saving target for the marketing department in the example may well involve the development of personal skills such as negotiation, costing and budgeting, but the primary focus is on the achievement of the departmental objective, ie saving £200,000.

DEVELOPMENTAL TARGETS

Developmental targets on the other hand place the primary focus on developing the individual; they might relate to:

- learning a new skill;
- taking on more responsibility;
- improving a particular aspect of the individual's performance;
- increasing knowledge;
- developing interpersonal skills, etc.

The easiest way of checking whether a target is really a developmental target is to ask whether the person will take the view that 'there is something in achieving this target for me'. The individual must have a vested interest in achieving the target; it will give something of personal value. You might like to consider the developmental targets in Figure 5.3 and think of a target for your own job which you would see as developmental.

Developmental targets by definition serve the purpose of developing a skill, knowledge or ability in an area where it does not currently exist or, if it does, where there is room for improvement. The implications of this are that an individual might interpret the target in one of two ways, either as an implied or overt criticism of current ability or as an opportunity to develop and improve their repertoire of skills. This will depend very much on how the process of target setting is handled and the tone of the discussion between the manager and subordinate; this is discussed in the next chapter.

Type	Target	How to achieve	Success criteria
Supervisory	Take supervisory responsibility for the two clerical staff in the department.	Coaching and guidance from departmental manager over next three months. Attendance on off-job supervisory training course.	Minimal amount of day-to-day supervision needed. No major problems needing managerial intervention.
Technical	Develop spreadsheet skills.	Attend relevant training course. To be allocated reports which demand the setting up of spreadsheets.	Able to set up spreadsheets for management reports. Effective data manipulation.
Managerial	Improve presentation skills.	Practise by giving informal presentations in departmental meetings. Attend in-company presentations skills training course.	Able to prepare and deliver presentations to external departments and outside the company without assistance by the end of the year.

Figure 5.3 Examples of developmental targets

SUCCESS CRITERIA

You will notice that for the targets shown in Figure 5.3 there is a column headed 'success criteria'. The success criteria establish at the target setting stage how it will be known at the review stage whether the target has been met or how well it has been met. By considering the subject of assessment at the start, review will be easier for both manager and subordinate and there is less likely to be disagreement because each had differing views of what was expected. It is especially important to build clear success criteria into developmental targets because it is less easy to include the type of numerical measure that is often found in quantitative targets. We will look at the subject of assessment in more detail in Chapter 6.

A useful approach when trying to determine success criteria for a particular target is to ask 'What should happen if the target is met?' The checklist in Figure 5.4 suggests a number of considerations which, if built in at the outset, will provide focus in working towards the target and help ease the process of assessment.

Method	Example
Cost	reduce costs to x
Speed	be able to operate at x speed
Deadlines	achieve the target in x months
Accuracy	achieve a certain level of accuracy
Number of mistakes	reduce the number of mistakes to x
Whether a task is achieved	has the job actually been done?
Knowledge level	knowledge can be tested
Skill level	observe someone doing it or test them
Change in behaviour	observe changed interpersonal skills
Amount of supervision needed	can they do the job alone?

Figure 5.4 Methods of measurement – a checklist

TOP-DOWN SUPPORT – BOTTOM-UP DEVELOPMENT

In a study of target setting in a number of organizations, Kane and Freeman (1986/7) identified three models of target setting: the democratic, the autocratic and the laissez-faire. This framework can help us think through some of the key issues in target setting generally and is summarized in Figure 5.5.

Equally we could apply this model to all sorts of initiatives which might be introduced to an organization. If you know of target setting or performance appraisal schemes which have been introduced to an organization you might like to consider which model most accurately describes the way they were introduced.

Research has consistently shown that when there is participation in decision making regarding target setting from lower levels, useful information that is known to subordinates is passed upwards and decisions result in

Autocratic model	Top management decides on targets and imposes them downwards.
Democratic model	Top management recommends targets which are agreed jointly with staff: target setting is a two-way process.
Laissez-faire model	Top management has lost interest in the system and leaves managers to set what become vague targets.

Figure 5.5 Three models of target setting

increased productivity. Senior level support for the target setting process is vital but participation is also critical in order to give credibility and an example or role model for others to follow (see Rogers and Hunter, 1991).

What we can learn from this is that on the one hand, managers should support and indeed become involved in the whole process of setting targets but, on the other, care should be taken to make sure subordinates have an input into deciding the subject matter and the success criteria of the targets they will be working towards. In the next chapter we look at the sequence of events in the target setting process and ways of ensuring employees have a real part to play in target setting.

REINFORCING ORGANIZATIONAL MESSAGES

We recommend that a set of targets for one person should focus on a maximum of six issues. Managers and individuals should attempt to identify the key areas of the job where achievement or improvement will have most impact. There should be a balance between targets which will contribute to organizational or departmental goals and those which develop the individual. This is where there is a real opportunity to ensure that targets will help both the person working towards the targets and his or her manager.

For example, if the department needs to improve communications with another, this rather vague aim can be brought down to a very practical level by identifying specific ways that one person can contribute to this departmental objective. This might be expressed in the following way:

Improve communications with the site services department by involving their staff in our departmental meetings when appropriate and by increasing the amount of face-to-face contact through informal visits rather than relying so heavily on written memos.

Equally there may be overall organizational themes which can be reinforced through effective target setting. Some examples would be:

- improve awareness of company performance;
- improve service to customers;
- do not walk past poor quality;
- improve use of latest technology;
- present a certain image to external contacts;
- increase the level of effective communication both downwards and upwards;
- do more 'management by wandering around';
- reduce the amount of unnecessary paperwork.

By including a target which relates to an organizational concern it is possible to reinforce some of the key cultural messages and this is a particularly effective way of helping to introduce change in thinking and behaviour on a broad basis. Of course it is essential to ensure the messages are correct and there would need to be some lead from the most senior level in this respect.

The secret to introducing organizational change is to start by changing the behaviour of individuals and to ensure that on certain issues there is a measure of consistency. This will in turn provide role models for others and establish 'how things are done round here'. Others are then more likely to adjust or adopt appropriate attitudes, and so cultural norms are more easily established.

USING TARGETS TO BREED SUCCESS

The term 'success criteria' referred to earlier is carefully and deliberately chosen. The emphasis is on individuals aiming to meet or exceed the target and the manager giving support for the same reason. All too often the focus is on not achieving the target and employees build up fears surrounding what will happen if the target is not met. What this means in terms of target setting is that every target should be achievable but stretching. This calls for careful judgement on the part of the trainer, the manager and the individual; obviously, what is easy for one person might be quite difficult for another. This will depend on a number of factors such as:

- experience
- existing knowledge
- enthusiasm
- fear
- confidence
- apparent relevance (face value)
- training
- education

Tom Peters (1989) sums up this subject perfectly in his book *Thriving on Chaos*:

> Put a 5 foot 10 inch person into 6 feet 3 inches of water, and odds are he'll learn to swim. He may sputter and spit a bit, but he can always hop up off the bottom and get air. Put that same person in 7 feet 4 inches of water and you may have a dead body on your hands.

It might feel slightly uncomfortable for the person trying to achieve the target but only by moving into new fields and pushing back the normal 'zone of comfort' will there be any real development. This is likely to lead to an upward cycle of success as shown in the lower section of Figure 5.6. If the target is considered totally unachievable, however, it is likely to lead to a dead-end and failure as shown by the upper part of Figure 5.6.

How realistic the targets are will depend largely on the climate created by the manager and the organization. This is where the models explained earlier can help. If the climate suggested by the democratic model for target setting is created then it is quite likely that the individual will suggest over-ambitious success criteria or timescales and the managerial role is to tone them down to become more realistic and achievable.

If, however, it is felt by employees that the system of target setting is purely a top-management mechanism for control, as suggested by the autocratic model, then employees are more likely to attempt to 'play the system' by ensuring that targets are set at an easily attainable level.

One way of creating a healthy climate is for the manager to demonstrate that the targets call for a two-way commitment: on the one hand the individual will work towards achievement of the target, on the other the manager will help the individual to achieve the target in whatever way possible. The checklist in Figure 5.7 provides examples of how the manager might help his or her staff work towards the achievement of a target.

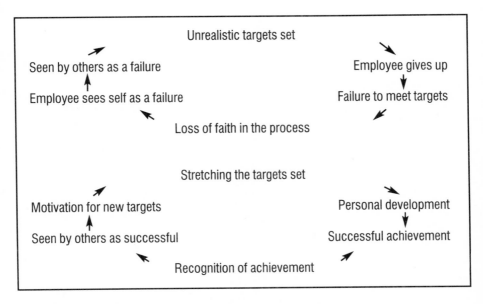

Figure 5.6 Setting achievable but stretching targets

- Coaching – for skills development
- Opening doors – facilitating senior level, specialist or external contacts
- Placements and secondments
- Freeing up time for prioritization of target area work
- Inclusion on circulation lists
- Sponsorship on training courses and conferences
- Mentoring
- Allocation of budgets
- Delegation of responsibility and authority
- Regular ongoing support and guidance

Figure 5.7 Target setting as a two-way process – the manager's commitment

There are no hard and fast rules regarding exactly how to word a target but as has been shown there are a number of ground rules which need to be applied to ensure that targets are realistically set and that they will prove motivating for the employee and beneficial for the organization. Finally, in this chapter we provide examples of many targets for different job roles based on actual targets set in organizations which have realized the benefits of effective target setting.

EXAMPLE TARGETS

Managerial Targets

Time management

Acquire and develop personal organization skills to improve productivity and performance. Should be able to plan personal and external time and resources to meet the requirements of the job.

Skills and knowledge to be developed by attending an off-job time-management course and subsequent development of time-management techniques and a personal planning diary system.

Success will be measured by ability to prioritize urgent and important work and a decrease in the number of crises occurring over the next six months.

Staff management

Demonstrate staff-management skill by being able to schedule staff to match workload on a weekly basis, taking due care to allocate staff according to experience and expertise as well as providing opportunities for staff development through on- and off-job training.

Schedules of staff loading to be kept and a review of the skills profile of staff to be compared with current status in nine months' time.

Training

Prepare an on-job training package which will help introduce new members of staff to the department by covering issues such as key personnel, working practices, terms and conditions and initial on-job training. Methods should be varied and may include written and verbal material. Publication of the agreed package within the next three months to be followed by a pilot trial over the following three months.

Recruitment

Recruit a sales manager for the sales department by drawing up a job description and personnel specification in discussion with the personnel department. Prepare and implement a plan for attracting a field of candidates; manage the selection process and recruit a suitable candidate by the end of the year. Costs to be monitored with the objective of remaining within budget.

Communications Targets

Cross-functional communication

Improve effective communication between the production department and engineering department by establishing regular meetings and developing informal communication methods. Engineering department should be made aware of production problems where they relate to design matters and this will be monitored by seeking a reduction in the number of post-production redesign problems over the next year.

Presentation skills

Develop effective presentation skills by attending the in-company presentations training course and through a programme of structured experience over the coming year which will progressively increase exposure to presentation situations.

Should be able to deliver customer presentations to company standard without assistance or supervision by the end of the year.

Team briefing

Introduce team briefing to the department and ensure that it becomes a valuable means of facilitating upward and downward communication. Practise team briefing for the department as a model for supervisors to follow and coach supervisors in how to brief their own staff.

Success will be measured by considering the number and quality of enquiries upwards and by checking that the core brief messages are understood by junior staff after nine months.

Administrative Targets

Administrative procedures

Design and agree with the relevant parties a flow diagram of the administrative system that should be adopted for the purchase of equipment and materials. This should take account of current practice and areas for future development or change.

The system should be agreed with the departmental manager within the next two months and then all staff in the department should be briefed on the system. Operation of the system should be continuously monitored and reviewed three months after instigation. Suggestions for further development should then be made. Success will be measured by looking at how workable the system is and whether there is a reduction in the number of supply problems.

Personal computing skills

Become familiar with and competent in the use of the software packages currently used in the department by attendance at an off-job course and through on-job coaching and self development over the next two months.

Should be able to access, set up and manipulate word-processed documents, spreadsheets and databases from raw data without supervision within four months.

Targets for Specific Functions

Technical skills

Improve technical skills in the field of data communications with the objective of being able to install and maintain new applications packages and to respond effectively to helpdesk enquiries within nine months.

To help in the achievement of this target attendance at relevant seminars and external product promotions will be encouraged as will inclusion on the circulation lists for relevant technical journals.

Finance

Control the annual budgeting and forecasting process for the company ensuring that adequate instructions are issued to budget holders in a timely fashion so that the company budget can be presented to the board in an acceptable format. Review budget proposals with departmental managers in advance of board level budget meeting and communicate subsequently agreed budgets.

This is to take place for the forthcoming financial year and success will be measured by considering the smooth running and timeliness of the budget preparation and review process.

Personnel

Improve the organization's image in the recruitment market place by providing a quicker response to applicants. The target is to reduce by half the average length of time taken to respond to applicants between:
1 initial application and regret or offer of interview;
2 interview and offer or regret.

This is to be achieved for the forthcoming recruitment round.

Organizational Targets

Flexibility

Demonstrate willingness to operate within the organization's objective of achieving flexibility in terms of performance of targets and working times. Should be prepared to carry out a range of different tasks which will vary according to workload and should be prepared to vary working hours to suit workload. When being asked to operate in new areas should be willing to undertake appropriate training. Review progress in nine months' time.

Business Process Reengineering

Introduce BPR concepts and practices to the organization by liaising with external consultants and senior management internally to set up a programme of initial workshops for all employees. This is to be delivered within 12 months. Should enable all senior and middle management to participate in the delivery of workshops to staff in their own areas.

ACTIVITY

Consider the following questions in relation to:

- your own job;
- your subordinate's job;
- someone in a different department.

In what areas of the job is it possible to set quantitative targets?
What would be an appropriate developmental target?
Try to write down these targets identifying output statements and success criteria.

6

Target Setting and Review

SUMMARY

In this chapter we will consider the review stage of the target setting initiative. It is suggested that a key to trouble-free review of targets is to build standards and measures into the original targets at the design stage. We also suggest that it is important to consider links with the rewards system and to clarify the relationship between the targets and the whole job.

We offer a method for weighting targets and emphasize the importance of self- review and continuous review. A model with recommended timescales is shown covering the various steps from target setting to review.

It is important to ensure that the 'front-end loaded' nature of the target setting process is understood throughout the organization, with the emphasis on establishing success criteria and means of assessment at the target setting rather than review stage. All employees need to be encouraged to accept ownership for their targets and to see the potential benefits in terms of personal development rather than viewing target setting as a passive process which is imposed from the top down.

So far we have established the importance of laying the foundation for the successful implementation of target setting in an organization by identifying the links with existing human resource systems and anticipating the major functional and cultural implications. By anticipating the likely objections and hurdles to be overcome during implementation, success is more likely than if one simply attempts to impose the system or imports a system from an external source. In the last chapter we looked at the specifics of how to set a target and some of the useful ground rules to ensure a target is measurable at the review stage. Here we will provide a framework and recommended timescale covering the full cycle from target setting through to the review stage including the vital interim steps.

Again there are a number of ground rules which are recommended and can be applied whatever the detailed nature of the procedures and paperwork of the organization. Review of progress against targets is often the most contentious and problematic aspect which those responsible for implementing target setting encounter and, as with the introduction of target setting, consideration of some of the common objections and pitfalls will help prepare the ground for success.

PREPARATION FOR REVIEW WHEN TARGETS ARE SET

The best advice with regard to the review stage suggests front-end loaded effort starting long before the review itself. By discussing the review of targets when actually setting them it is possible to clarify success criteria and to distinguish between unacceptable, acceptable and exceptional performance. Many individuals will feel that they are disadvantaged at the review stage by, for instance, the documentation which they have to use. Often they are quite justified in feeling that documentation could be improved and that it is constraining. It might be felt that if a review system requires a rating of, say, exceptional/acceptable/unacceptable then insufficient consideration is given to the details of performance against a target: managers simply tick a box based on fairly arbitrary judgement. For the manager and employee there is an effective way of working round such a system by describing at the target setting stage what the outcome might be for each of the ratings. Examples are given of how this might work in practice in Figure 6.1.

The subject of the target in this example is a managerial one which combines qualitative measures with a degree of quantitative assessment, but without overemphasis on numerical measures. When preparing for the target setting discussion both parties would benefit from thinking through these issues in advance. By asking the question 'What would be the circumstances and outcomes across a range of performance assessments?' the assessment process will be much more straightforward than if both parties make assumptions that the other person will be working from the same frame of reference and that there is no need to discuss assessment at such an early stage. Research by Locke and Latham (1990) found that in target setting there is normally a tendency to show leniency at the evaluation stage and this can be minimized if goals are defined in specific terms.

Subject of target

For a manager to introduce a change management initiative which aims to improve communications and productivity over a period of one year.

Exceptional performance

Performance will be considered exceptional if the initiative is fully embedded in the organization and a comparison of results for the site-wide attitude survey conducted at the start and end of the year reveals at least a doubling of positive responses against all four categories of question (commitment, training and development, human resource procedures and practices).

Furthermore, a programme of associated training should be completed at supervisor and middle-management level and evidence should be provided that problem-solving groups are self sustaining on at least three production lines and have progressed at least one successful idea each through to the implementation stage.

A random sample of staff will be expected to be able to explain satisfactorily key management concepts and to quote the organization's mission statement.

Acceptable performance

An improvement is identified when comparing the response to the employee attitude surveys.

Training programmes at supervisory and management level should have commenced and problem solving groups should have been established.

All staff should be aware of the organization's mission statement and in a random sample some should be able to explain the key concepts of change management.

Unacceptable performance

There is no visible improvement in the response to the employee attitude survey. Training programmes will not have taken place and problem-solving groups will not have been established, or if they have, they will have been allowed to fall into disuse through lack of proper support.

In a random sample of staff none will be able to explain satisfactorily the concepts of change management or will be aware of the organization's mission statement.

Figure 6.1 Description of outcomes against a rating system

BALANCING TARGETS WITH OTHER RESPONSIBILITIES

The principle behind target setting is that by concentrating on the most important parts of the job, individuals will know where to apply effort which will make the most impact on the business. It was demonstrated by the nineteenth-century Italian economist Pareto that 80 per cent of the Italian population owned 20 per cent of the nation's wealth; it was discovered that this ratio could be applied in a number of different contexts. For instance 80 per cent of the costs of a product might be found in 20 per cent of the components or 80 per cent of the profits of an organization might come from just 20 per cent of its products or services. Similarly, the Pareto principle might be applied to the job role and targets: 80 per cent of the impact an individual makes comes from just 20 per cent of the job responsibilities.

Selection of the target areas might be based on, for example:

- linking the job to organizational objectives;
- developing managerial skills;
- developing interpersonal skills;
- improving ability to perform current tasks;
- preparing for the future;
- improving communications;
- broadening knowledge;
- achieving qualifications; or
- generating income, sales, fees, etc.

While it is important to attempt to identify the key 20 per cent of responsibilities, tasks or skill areas which will make 80 per cent of the impact, it is equally critical to recognize that of the remaining 80 per cent there will be tasks or responsibilities, which, if ignored, will reflect on the overall ability of the employee, and could ultimately affect the tenability of the position. This suggests that while assessment should focus primarily on achievement of targets, credit should also be given for achievement in areas where targets are not established. If there is a job description this will identify the 'whole picture' in terms of areas of responsibility and targets to be achieved. Job descriptions, though, do not necessarily highlight the priorities and methods for meeting targets and deadlines; these need to be agreed on an individual basis through the target setting process.

Areas of the job which are not linked to targets but form an important part of the 80 per cent could include routine tasks, regular activities, aspects of work completed by a number of people and maintenance type responsibilities.

Remuneration schemes sometimes reward only achievement as judged against targets at the expense of ignoring other parts of the job. This can have a highly demotivational effect on those employees whose roles include a high degree of maintenance type activity. For such employees it may be appropriate to build some of the maintenance type activities into targets and to consider setting some common targets for a group of similar job holders, for example:

Maintain an efficient filing system which enables ease and speed of access to current and accurate information by users.

Demonstrate willingness to assist other operatives on their production line when your own line is not busy. Utilize assistance from operatives from other lines when your own line is particularly under pressure.

Maintain a consistently courteous and helpful approach to customers and act upon their enquiries by promptly referring to the appropriate manager if you are unable to resolve issues alone.

Some organizations relate rewards to achievements through an annual or six-monthly bonus system and the achievement of the '80 per cent' type activities through the salary review. The emphasis in this sort of rewards system is on recognizing that if targets are achieved this demonstrates achievement over and above the baseline of expected responsibilities. In that continued achievement against these activities is not predictable in the future it is considered inappropriate to guarantee continual payment and to reward such achievement through the regular salary payments system. This can prove to be a motivational strategy but if this is at the expense of extrinsic recognition of efforts in the '80 per cent' type areas this can become a cause of dissent and dissatisfaction. The way that this is often handled is to include in the salary review an element which reflects continued good performance in the 80 per cent areas. This might form one element in the salary review calculation along with consideration of, for example, organizational results, trading conditions, local employment-market conditions, functional employment-market conditions and the current rate of inflation. The boxed exercise at the end of this chapter will help you to separate out these 80 per cent areas from other responsibilities.

Obviously reward systems vary considerably across organizations but it is critical to consider exactly how the achievement of results will be linked to rewards through remuneration in advance of, or in conjunction with, the implementation of a target setting initiative. In line with research which has found that performance-related pay does not necessarily correlate with organizational bottom-line results (IPM, 1992), some organizations are now repositioning the target setting and review process to distance it from pay reviews and rewards. This gives the advantage of being able to generate a more healthy two-way discussion about performance and personal development.

Sometimes it is obvious that while, say, six targets have been identified for a particular position, they do not all carry equal value in terms of either impact on the organization and individual, or effort required to achieve them. In this case it is appropriate to prioritize and weight them accordingly. Weighting will depend on the relative value of issues such as:

- importance to the business, department, section;
- urgency, speed required;
- importance of personal development;
- imminence of future changes; and
- technological developments.

As with any weighting system it is possible to introduce sophisticated statistical techniques and the danger is that the system becomes an end in itself rather than a means to an end. A practical approach would be to rank each target area according to urgency and importance as in the worked example in Figure 6.2.

Twenty points to be distributed for importance and urgency across target subjects. 'Total' column is from a maximum of 40 points. 'Weighting' column is 'total' figure times 2.5 to give a total of 100 (per cent).

Target subject	Importance	Urgency	Total	Weighting
Develop a new admin system	1	4	5	12.5
Improve communications	6	6	12	30.0
Improve production methods	4	3	7	17.5
Form new project teams	5	1	6	15.0
Presentation skills	2	1	3	7.5
Recruit new team members	2	5	7	17.5
Total	20	20	40	100.0

Figure 6.2 Weighting of targets

The advantage of such a system is that there is agreement on the weighting and value of specific targets as early as the target setting stage. This means that employees will know where to focus their efforts and which targets to prioritize in terms of timescales once they have been set. Employees can then be given the discretion to decide on how to achieve their targets. This sort of weighting system also means that there will not be any surprises when it comes to the assessment of achievements with employees discovering that their managers had different views on the relevant importance of targets.

ENCOURAGING SELF-REVIEW AND CONTINUAL REVIEW

Just as it is fundamental in target setting to encourage employees to identify their own priorities when devising targets as a means of encouraging ownership, it is equally important to place the initial emphasis on the individual when reviewing progress and achievements. There are several advantages to beginning the review with the employee's reflections rather than passing judgement from on high.

First, the tone of the target setting initiative will be seen to be participative rather than autocratic and employees are far more likely to be committed to the agreement regarding outcomes and achievements. Second, it makes it much easier for managers to open up a constructive discussion on shortfalls or problem areas where targets have not been satisfactorily achieved. Interestingly, most employees will be more critical of themselves than their manager would be and often the manager will have the more pleasant task of raising the self-review in an upward direction. When the review process starts with the managers presenting their opinion of the performance of subordinates, there might be one of two potentially damaging reactions: there could be a heated and emotional disagreement, or, on the other hand, the employee may feel less inclined to take issue with areas of disagreement and the opportunity for open discussion will be stifled.

It is also crucial to recognize that the review of targets is not a one-off and final event conducted at the end of the period for achievement. Employees should be encouraged to continually monitor their own progress against targets and the manager should conduct informal interim reviews throughout the period in question. This will mean that the emphasis of the final review is on finalizing and pulling together issues already discussed in interim reviews.

If there have been interim reviews and a continual discussion of progress towards targets with ongoing support from management in helping the employee to achieve them then unpleasant surprises at the final review are less likely. Continual review also provides the opportunity to agree modifications to targets if it is accepted that the original parameters have changed significantly due to circumstances beyond the employee's control and the target has become inappropriate or unrealistic.

TIMESCALES FROM TARGET SETTING TO REVIEW

When setting targets there is a danger that, in considering deadlines, all the targets will be set to be achieved by the major review date, that is usually after six or twelve months. The problem with this approach is that the employee will find that as the date for review looms there are a number of major activities which have been put off and overall success is less likely than if dates for completion of targets had been spread throughout the year. When deciding on the priority of targets it will be apparent in considering the aspect of urgency and demands on the employee that some targets can be set for completion earlier than others.

At an organizational level it is necessary to decide whether the main review of targets is going to be held for all staff at the same time of year or at different times for each employee. Clearly the advantages of linking review to individually related dates, such as the anniversary of commencing employment or birthdays, will spread the administrative load on the organization and departmental managers fairly evenly throughout the year. This also will help to encourage the view that the review of targets is a continual process which should be built into the everyday activities of management. By reviewing targets at the same time of year for all employees, however, it is more likely that, due to the pressure this puts on managers in coping with the sheer number of reviews to be completed, the process will be considered more administrative than developmental.

Another advantage of spreading reviews for employees throughout the year is that they will be less likely to place quite so much emphasis on comparing the results of their own review with those of their peers. This will mean that more valuable judgements can be drawn as the individual compares performance and achievements against previous skills and abilities.

Figure 6.3. shows a schematic covering recommended timescales for the entire process from target setting through to review. Obviously precise timescales will vary between organizations but the schematic suggests some key stages.

Figure 6.3 suggests that the first stage of the entire process should be an introductory discussion between the manager and the subordinate to explain the aims of target setting and the system as operated in the organization. At this stage it is necessary to explain the order of the target setting process and to show the subordinate the associated documentation and how it will be used. Both parties should finally agree to consider broad subject areas which will form the basis for more detailed discussion and development of targets. Ideally both the manager and subordinate will have had some training in the skills of target setting before reaching this stage but in reality this is not always the case. If there has been no training for the subordinate then it will be helpful for the manager to provide a briefing, and if responsible for a group of staff then a workshop for the departmental team can be a useful way of generating a discussion and a full understanding of the most important issues. The subject of training and target setting skills is covered in Chapter 8.

A reasonable time lapse between the original discussion and the main target setting meeting is about two weeks. This will enable the subordinate to become more familiar with the process and the documentation and to give sufficient serious thought to target areas which will be of personal as well as departmental and organizational benefit. It may also be appropriate to refer upwards to the manager during this pre-target setting period to discuss ideas on subjects for targets. Even when this does not occur it is surprising how often both parties will identify similar areas upon which to base targets.

The next stage is for the target setting meeting to take place and sufficient time should be allocated for a constructive discussion on level terms. A suggested structure for this meeting is to start by agreeing the six or so subjects which will form the basis of separate targets; here it is possible to check that there is a balance between different types of target such as technical, managerial, personal, developmental and organizational. On comparing target subjects it is likely that some suggested subjects can be linked with others in an attempt to reduce the number of targets to a maximum of around six.

The next stage of the discussion should focus on defining success criteria, timescales and how the manager will help the subordinate to achieve the targets agreed. Some managers like to complete the relevant documentation at this stage, while others prefer to do this outside the context of the target setting meeting. The major drawback of completing documentation during the meeting is that free-flowing conversation tends to be cramped as paperwork takes over.

Allowing a short period of time between the meeting and the completion of the documentation will also provide the employee with the opportunity to think about the targets which have been discussed without feeling under pressure. Providing the opportunity for subsequent refinement of targets before finally signing them off also helps to encourage ownership.

When actually signing off the relevant documentation it should be made clear that both parties are entering into a two-way commitment; the employee will work towards the target and the manager will make resources and expertise available to help.

The ongoing review meetings which can be carried out at, say, monthly intervals do not need to be extended discussions. If there is continual informal support and review of progress then these will simply be a discussion of views, problems and plans for progressing towards the individual targets. For the manager this is clearly another occasion where assistance can be offered to facilitate success for the subordinate.

The final review is really a summary of all reviews to date and an overall discussion of success as measured against the original criteria. It also coincides with the timing of the development of new targets, some of which will be identified as evolving naturally from the old ones.

Again the principle of allowing some time before signing the overall review will allow the employee to consider, alone, whether the review as discussed at the meeting is fair and it will allow time for completion of relevant company review documents.

DISTINGUISHING TARGETS FROM OTHER RESPONSIBILITIES

1 Starting with a job description if you have one, or starting afresh, list all the tasks and responsibilities which feature in your job.
2 Categorize these into goals, key areas, and specific tasks.
3 Draw out subjects which you consider important enough to form the basis for targets and again list these separately.
4 Add to the original list of targets additional subjects for targets by considering the future of the job and the organization and your own development needs to achieve personal goals.

You should now have separated key targets, that is, the 20 per cent of your responsibilities which will generate 80 per cent of the impact.

Activity	Timing	Objective
Introductory discussion; manager and subordinate		Outline aims of target setting Benefits to individual and organization Paperwork involved Both agree to consider key areas for targets
	2 weeks maximum interval	
Main target setting meeting		Discuss and decide on broad target areas
	1 week maximum interval	
Completion of written documentation by manager and subordinate Signing off of targets		Final agreement of targets Clarification of two-way commitment Manager to explain how subordinate will be helped Subordinate to agree to work towards targets Agree timescales
Continued monitoring and review of targets	6 months	
Summary review		Summary review of achievement against targets Forward planning of future targets
	2 days	
Signing off reviewed targets		Confirm agreement with review

Figure 6.3 Schematic of the target setting process

7

The Interpersonal Skills of Target Setting and Review

SUMMARY

In this chapter we focus on the communication skills which need to be developed in order to cope with the interpersonal aspects of target setting and review. Organizations should be continually seeking to develop the interpersonal skills of employees through direct training interventions and informal methods such as coaching, briefings and the provision of information. In particular we consider:

- listening;
- feedback;
- empathy;
- questioning; and
- confrontation.

We then look at how perception becomes distorted and how this can affect judgement of performance.

There are a number of interpersonal skills which need to be practised and developed when setting targets with staff. Refining some of these skills is a subtle and continuous process which will come with experience and effort. It is possible to identify the basic components of such skills and consciously to develop them through a structured approach to on- and off-job training. The challenge is to facilitate the development of these skills throughout the organization through a combination of formalized training interventions and continual coaching.

The specific interpersonal skills we will look at here can be applied in several managerial contexts but are especially relevant when it comes to target setting and reviewing progress against targets. Ironically, they tend to be the communication skills which we have to practise earliest in our development and use the most but are not taught as part of our general education. We will consider the skills of listening and questioning and how we can combine these to convey an empathetic and objective approach to target setting and review. We will also identify the component parts of effective feedback, which are of particular relevance to the target review process. It is also important to be aware of some of the natural human failings we are susceptible to in processing information, making judgements about others and the various ways in which our perception tends to become distorted. By developing an understanding of our limitations and prejudices and adjusting behaviour accordingly it is possible to take a more objective approach, which is the key to successful target setting and review.

COMMUNICATION SKILLS

Target setting should be positioned clearly as a two-way communication process involving the manager and individual and as such there are a number of potential blocks to effective communication which should be avoided to ensure maximum gain is experienced by both parties. It is particularly important to consider the nature of the communication process as it involves a superior/subordinate relationship and the intention is to discuss what is actually a very personal subject. The danger with target setting and review is that the discussion revolves around the technical aspects of the job or task and a work-centred discussion ensues rather than one focusing on how the individual will achieve the target. The task-centred rather than person-centred approach is especially likely to occur when the nature of the industry or job is technical and it is relatively easy to avoid the difficult aspect of discussing personal performance, which usually means dealing with emotion and sometimes handling conflict and confrontation.

There are some commonsense suggestions which will ease the communication process and are more likely to encourage open discussion; these are covered in the checklist in Figure 7.1.

There are a number of issues here which the manager needs to consider, both in target setting and review. In the worst scenario the target setting interview or the target review interview takes place as something fitted in among other supposedly more important pressures and the meeting is

Environment	Noise, seating, heating, lighting, interruptions.
Timing	Keep to the agreed date, time of day, time of week, amount of time.
Assumptions	Level of knowledge, level of skill, confidence, attitude.
Prejudices	Assuming others will feel the same as us, our own strengths are not necessarily those of others.
Status	Be aware of the status relationships.
Value others	Everyone has a right to their own views.
Non-verbal	Back up words with the appropriate non-verbal communication, tone, posture, expressions.
Verbal	Be aware of value judgements, and emotionally charged words, eg 'brilliant', 'hopeless'.
Withholding	
information	Question whether it needs to be withheld.
Confrontation	Do not avoid it, channel it constructively.
Listening	Practise active listening.
Questioning	Use questions to demonstrate listening.
Empathy	Put yourself in the other person's shoes.
Silence	Do not fear silence, use it effectively, allow thinking time.
Feedback	Give constructive feedback.

Figure 7.1 Checklist for improving communications in target setting and review

subject to interruptions and is often rearranged for another time. This marginalizes what to the individual is a very important activity.

It is worth considering the most appropriate time of day for the discussion: this will differ across organizations but managers should try to find a time which will allow for overrun if necessary. It is easy for the manager to make incorrect assumptions about how a task is viewed by the subordinates regarding for example, degree of difficulty and confidence in approaching it. It is a mistake to steamroll the imposition of a target. It is important to show empathy with employees and to find out how they feel about a particular subject and to attempt to summarize their underlying feelings both when setting targets and when reviewing them.

It should be recognized that as the target setting and review interviews are usually coordinated by managers with their subordinates, there may be natural barriers which inhibit free-flowing conversation. This problem can be countered by creating a climate of mature and constructive conversation rather than judgement from above. On occasions it will be necessary to accept that confrontation, however, is inevitable and indeed requisite. If an employee has clearly not performed this cannot be ignored at the review stage. If there has been regular ongoing conversation about performance on an informal basis throughout the year there is less likely to be confrontation as there will be few surprises for the employee being reviewed. When there are disagreements though, the manager should attempt to identify the root cause; it may be the case that the employee being reviewed has information, previously unknown to the manager, as to why targets were not met.

Some of the specific skills worth developing in more depth are those of listening, empathizing, questioning and giving feedback.

LISTENING

As an interpersonal skill listening is often confused with hearing. It is possible, for instance, to hear background music without thinking about the words being sung or their meaning. This is different to listening actively which is a skill we can consciously develop. People avoid listening for a variety of reasons; for instance, it may be that we do not hear what we do not want to hear. This is a defence mechanism which helps us avoid a problem or reality. This has serious implications in the context of reviewing progress against targets for both the manager and the subordinate being reviewed. Both parties may not actually understand what the other party is saying. It is also common for people to avoid listening when the other person's views contradict their own ideas and preconceptions. This again presents a number of dangers when reviewing targets. Also, it is natural to avoid listening due to information overload; in other words, it is just not possible to think about all the issues being discussed at once. Listening skills can actually be broken down into specific techniques; some of these are explained in Figure 7.2.

One of the most difficult and advanced aspects of active listening is showing empathy. This really means understanding not just how a person feels but why they feel like they do. By demonstrating empathy when reviewing targets it is much more likely that constructive conversation will follow. Showing empathy does not mean talking about yourself or attempting to impose solutions. It is about listening to, and understanding, the other person's position and feelings before offering ideas and working towards solutions.

Technique	Example
Non-verbal communication	Head nod, tone, eye contact, facial expression.
Summarizing	'So in summary you believe you have achieved the target for the following reasons . . .'
Repeating key words	Echoing back key words and generating more output from the speaker.
Encouragement	'That is very interesting, tell me more . . . , 'Mmm', 'Uh-huh'.
Reflect back feelings	'So you are clearly pleased with your performance'.
Pauses	Silence can be used to buy time in which to prepare thoughts and allow the other person to think through responses; establish from early on that silence is acceptable.

Figure 7.2 Active listening techniques

In the empathizing exercise shown you might like to offer an empathetic response to the three comments made by the employee who is being reviewed against the achievement of targets.

The responses suggested in the example may sound contrived and obviously there are many ways of offering an empathetic response, but the principle is important: demonstrate your understanding of the underlying feelings before moving on to proposed solutions or making judgements.

QUESTIONING

Just as listening is a vital skill which will come to the fore at the target setting and review stages, the skills of effective questioning are equally important. Effective questioning techniques can help when it comes to discussing potential target areas and when reviewing progress. The most useful types of question here are those that encourage self-review and draw on ideas from the individual rather than impose the views of the manager. Figure 7.3 gives some examples which might be appropriate in target setting and review.

EMPATHIZING WHEN REVIEWING TARGETS

Rephrase the following statements from the person you are reviewing to give an empathetic response which shows that you recognize and understand their underlying feelings.

1. It has just not been possible to achieve the target this year because of the problems with changing workload, the fact that my job role has increased due to losing staff. I never get a chance to concentrate on any one thing. I get pushed about by top management all the time and I have just about had enough.

2. It's great; this time last year I would never have thought that I could achieve so much and that I would be mixing with our customers on a regular basis. It is really exciting to be the main representative of the company at social events and I really get a buzz out of the public relations aspect of the job.

3. I never get consulted about the new recruits who join this section. The way I get to find out about anything is through gossip in the corridor and even then I am the last to hear. It seems everyone else knows what's happening. How do you expect me to meet targets if you do not let me know what is going on?

Examples of Inappropriate Responses

1. I know. I get fed up with the never-ending changes too. I don't know whether I am coming or going sometimes.
   (Inappropriate response because it focuses on the reviewer rather than the reviewee.)
2. You are clearly going places.
   (Inappropriate response because it moves the conversation on with an assumption about the future.)
3. Why don't you stop moaning and take a more positive outlook or you will never get anywhere.
   (Inappropriate response because it moves into the problem-solving stage without involving the other person; it suggests a solution.)

Examples of Empathetic Responses

1. It sounds like you are quite angry because of the changes which have been imposed on you.
2. You seem very pleased with the increased responsibilities you have been given.
3. It must be very frustrating to feel left out when it comes to communication about changes in staffing.

Target setting

1   What do you consider to be the most important aspects of your job?
2   What help do you need to ensure that you succeed in the future?
3   How could you measure your success?
4   In what ways is your role changing?
5   What are the external influences on your performance?
6   What are your special interest areas?
7   What technical aspects of your job are important?
8   What skills do you need to help you develop further?
9   What knowledge do you need to acquire?
10   What qualifications would help you for the future?
11   What are your short-term priorities and what are your medium and long-term goals?

Target review

1   How do you feel that you have performed against this target?
2   What areas are you pleased with?
3   What areas are you disappointed with?
4   What helped you to achieve this target?
5   How do you feel about the level of cooperation you have received when working towards this target?
6   In what ways has the target helped you to develop personal skills?
7   What technical skills have you developed?
8   What knowledge do you have now that you did not have before?
9   What do you consider to be your strengths/weaknesses?

Figure 7.3 Examples of questions to ask when setting and reviewing targets

FEEDBACK

Having encouraged self-review of performance against targets by the employee, the manager will need to offer feedback. Giving feedback is a skill in itself and there are a number of guidelines which need to be adhered to. Feedback should describe effective or ineffective behaviour rather than consist of sweeping generalizations or evaluative statements.

For example, it is more appropriate to state 'You have worked closely with your team and helped to integrate new members through the instigation of team meetings', than to say 'Great teamwork!' Similarly, rather than saying 'You are a hopeless leader', a more effective approach would be 'Your team leadership has suffered because you have not given sufficient time and emphasis to group activities using your staff'.

Effective feedback specifies or describes the behaviour and should focus on things that are capable of being modified. So, for example, it would be inappropriate to criticize an employee for failing to carry out a physical task fast enough if they are physically incapable of doing so. At a more subtle level the manager should be sensitive to the less obvious limitations of the individual.

CONFRONTATION

Inevitably there will be occasions when the individual has a perception of their own performance which is different from that of the manager and there may be confrontation. Clearly this will be less likely if the targets have been set according to the principles discussed earlier. When it does occur, though, confrontation needs to be managed and both parties should make explicit their own view and clarify differences in opinion. A useful procedure to follow when facing a confrontation situation is to:

1 accept that the other person currently has a different view;
2 identify the differences from your own view;
3 actively listen to check that you have understood correctly the other person's views – use rephrasing and summarizing techniques;
4 recognize the feelings in the other person; show empathy. Watch out for anger which tends to be accompanied by faster, louder or higher-pitched speech or aggressive language and posture;
5 recognize your own feelings and emotions; name them but differentiate feelings from facts;
6 do not move into attempting to solve the problem until differences on both sides have been discussed;
7 ask the other person to suggest some preferred solutions, and state your own; aim for a workable compromise.

There are, then, a number of techniques and skills which the effective manager needs to develop in order to be able to maximize the benefits of target setting and review. It is also helpful to be aware of ways in which our perception of others can be distorted; it is then possible to guard against these tendencies and maintain as objective and fair an approach as possible.

PERCEPTUAL DISTORTIONS

Attraction to Like

There is a natural tendency to be attracted to others who are similar to ourselves. Similarities might include, for example, appearance, common interests, strengths, background, gender, race, hobbies and sports. The danger here is that we confuse liking someone with making an objective appraisal of their performance.

Equally, there is a danger of rating a person down who does not carry out tasks or activities in the same way as oneself. It may be that the other person's approach is just as appropriate and achieves the same output but in a different way.

Halo and Horns Effect

There is a natural tendency to assume that if someone succeeds in one aspect of their life or behaviour they must be successful in all other areas of their life. Similarly, if someone has failed in one area we often assume that they will do so in every other respect. We place a figurative halo or a set of horns on their heads, hence the use of phrases such as 'black sheep', 'blue-eyed boy', and 'golden girl'. In evaluating performance it is important to measure achievement against the specific criteria originally agreed and not to fall into the trap of making assumptions based on irrelevant data or information.

Stereotypes

We are all susceptible to the dangers of stereotyping: making assumptions that a lot of other characteristics follow on from one aspect of a person's character. We fit people into the stereotypical image for that category of person. Stereotypes are based around a number of issues such as gender, race, religion, age and profession or occupation. It is, however, possible to make serious misjudgements about people because of the tendency to stereotype. Some examples of stereotypical assumptions are:

- women are less capable than men of performing physical duties;
- older people will not accept change;
- young people will enjoy lively activity;
- accountants are serious and conservative;
- manual workers cannot contribute to management decisions;
- the family man is not ambitious;

- marketing people are aggressive;
- religious people are calm and contented.

Looking at these statements logically it is obvious that we cannot and should not make such sweeping generalizations. It is particularly dangerous to make such judgements when considering what targets to set for staff and when evaluating performance against targets. Assessment must be based on observable and justifiable evidence.

Primacy and Recency Effect

In terms of the human memory and impressions, there is a tendency to be disproportionately affected by first impressions and the most recent event; these perceptual distortions are known as the primacy and recency effect. The implications when monitoring performance are that the manager may fail to review the whole period since the target was set and instead focus on, for instance, the initial teething problems or honeymoon period or the most recent success or failure.

ACTIVITY

Consider the performance of a member of staff or colleague and formulate a plan for giving effective feedback in an area where there is room for improvement or development.

Consider your own prejudices and the stereotypes which you are susceptible to. A useful way of approaching this is to recall when you say 'He or she is a typical ...'

Who do you know of in your organization who benefits from the halo effect or is a victim of the horns effect?

Part III

Training in Target Setting

8

Training Managers and Employees to Set Targets

SUMMARY

In this chapter we consider the importance of training when introducing target setting to an organization. Two examples of training intervention are shown: the half-day workshop, and the two-day off-job training course. We consider who to involve in training and methods of providing ongoing support beyond the initial training programme. We need to judge the method and depth of training that is appropriate for the organization and the two examples shown here are simply meant to provide ideas of different approaches. We provide guidance on how to deal with questions and barriers from delegates.

In Part I we considered the importance of viewing target setting in the historical context of developments in the field of performance management and we stressed the importance of recognizing the existing systems and the culture of the organization before attempting to introduce a target setting programme. In Part II we looked at the practicalities of target setting, that is how to set and review targets at an individual level and the relevance of core interpersonal skills.

It is now relevant to look at how to introduce target setting to the organization. Clearly it is self-defeating for the human resource or personnel specialist simply to design a system and impose it on the organization. It is essential to launch target setting with appropriate training which will serve two key purposes. First, training should address the subject of how target setting links with other related systems such as performance appraisal and performance-related pay. This also means that coverage of the practical steps of target setting is necessary. This will include the use of documentation, the reporting and monitoring system and timescales. Second, it is essential to offer the opportunity for practice and development of the key interpersonal skills identified in Chapter 7 and practice in designing example targets which conform to the ground rules for effective targets.

Focusing on these two issues, the system and the skills, will pave the way for successful implementation by enabling managers to raise their major concerns in the constructive forum of a training course or workshop. It is important to recognize these concerns from an early stage in order to help encourage managers to buy into the process. Development of knowledge and skills in target setting is in fact the easier part of training, whereas the development of appropriate attitudes is a longer-term project which must start at the launch stage.

Clearly there will be a cost associated with training in target setting and the options used by organizations range from the one-week residential programme through to half-day workshops on site, each with their associated scale of costs. Such costs need to be weighed against the projected costs of not training. For example, without training there are likely to be high costs in terms of dealing with managers on an individual basis to tackle problems as and when they arise, and the costs of coping with the fact that managers are likely to apply target setting in an inconsistent manner without training and the costs of dealing with staff who may become demotivated by what they perceive as a poorly implemented system.

Provision of target setting can be approached in two stages: first, the design of training, and second, the implementation of training. We will look at these aspects of training by suggesting two different types of training input: the short workshop and the off-job course. We will look at these in terms of method, timing and content.

The decision on the amount and type of training necessary will be determined by consideration of previous training given, existing skills and anticipation of attitudes towards target setting. If there has been a history of successful performance appraisal and the target setting initiative is simply intended to enhance the existing system, then it may be appropriate to provide short practical workshops on the site of the organization. On the other hand, if the organization has a history of performance appraisal and monitoring which has not been successful, overcoming attitude barriers may be a major issue. In this case it is often more appropriate to take managers off site for a residential programme over a period of at least two days. In terms of who designs and delivers training, again there are a number of choices. Players in target setting training might include training and development staff, personnel professionals, line managers and senior managers and external consultants. It may be relevant to involve all these parties in different capacities. At the design stage trainers should project-manage the development of training, drawing on other expertise from the personnel function and if possible involving line managers. It may be the case that external consultants are able to offer a breadth of experience and specialist expertise in performance management, but simply buying in 'off the shelf' training and performance appraisal systems without tailoring them to the needs of the organization is a sure way to generate problems at the implementation stage. A very powerful technique is to involve representatives from senior management in providing an input to training. This might take the form of an introductory input to explain from a senior-management perspective where target setting sits within the context of organizational goals and objectives.

At the design stage it is also crucial to consider how those who will not be involved in setting targets for others, but will be on the receiving end of target setting, will be trained. Options here include specific training for employees falling into this category or integration of such staff with managers and supervisors for training programmes which are covered on a department-by-department basis. A common mistake is to focus only on those who are setting targets for others. This is often at the expense of the person who is actually going to work towards achievement of the target. This is likely to engender a 'them and us' feeling and unlikely to generate a positive attitude towards target setting from the start.

Below are the two examples of training intervention. Obviously there are a number of other options available in terms of length of training and detailed content, but the examples show the two different approaches, the on-job and the off-job input.

MODEL FOR AN ON-JOB TARGET SETTING WORKSHOP

Objectives

To introduce the target setting initiative to managers and their staff so that they understand how the current system of performance appraisal has been developed to include target setting.

To develop target setting skills and provide an understanding of the ground rules relating to target setting.

Method

Facilitation of a three-hour workshop by a facilitator with the use of lecture, handouts and group exercises in target setting.

Timetable

Time	Content and method
9.00	Introduction to target setting initiative and the workshop.
9.15	Understanding of existing performance appraisal system – problems, pitfalls, benefits. Guided discussion.
9.45	Guidance on target setting through lecture and handouts. Delegates are asked to identify a subject for target setting which could be for their own job, their manager's job, their subordinate's job and practise the design of targets in pairs for presentation to the group.
10.15	Presentation of model targets to the group which will decide whether they meet the criteria established in the previous session. Group discussion.
11.00	Documentation and system issues such as timescale from target setting to review and the role of the personnel department. Explanation of follow-up support which is available for managers and provided by the personnel and training departments. Input with handouts.
11.30	Review of the workshop with an open forum for questions and answers. Action planning for target setting by departmental and sectional managers.
12.00	Close

MODEL FOR AN OFF-JOB RESIDENTIAL TRAINING COURSE

Objectives

To provide the opportunity for open discussion of target setting. To develop positive attitudes towards target setting and willingness among delegates to participate in the organization's target setting initiative after the training programme has been completed.

To develop the interpersonal skills associated with effective target setting and review and to increase knowledge of how to set targets.

Method

A two-day off-site training course which is coordinated and tutored by the training department with inputs from the personnel manager and the managing director. The course combines discussion, lectures and participative exercises. Delegates receive a briefing on course objectives and a timetable one week before attending the course.

Timetable

Time   Content and method

DAY ONE

9.00   Introduction to course content, objectives, style and methods. Discussion of hopes, fears and expectations for the course and the target setting initiative facilitated by the course leader.

9.45   Exercise in syndicate groups to consider how performance is currently measured and in what ways staff are given future direction. Followed up by plenary discussion.

10.45   Lecture on developments in the field of performance management supplemented with handouts and discussion.

11.45   Lecture and discussion on developments in the organization's performance-management system. Delivered by the personnel manager.

12.30   Lunch

1.30   Skills development exercises in syndicates facilitated by group tutors. Coverage of questioning skills, listening skills and feedback skills.

4.00   Lecture and discussion on the techniques of target setting, including ground rules for effective target setting and discussion of how targets can be set in specialist areas, eg technical, creative, service and administration functions.

4.30   Preparation for target setting exercise which will be conducted on day two. Delegates identify three different types of targets for their own position or their staff's – organizational, developmental and functional. Sharing of thoughts with other delegates.

5.30   Close

DAY TWO

9.00   Review of learning points from day one. Discussion facilitated by course tutor.

9.30   Preparation, in pairs, of targets by delegates. Exercise with guidance and support from tutors.

11.00   Presentation of targets to the plenary group by delegates. Delegates present their targets on flipcharts.

12.30   Lunch

1.30   Target setting in context – performance appraisal video. Video which demonstrates the application of target setting and performance appraisal in other organizations. (See page 154 for a list of recommended videos.)

2.00   Question and answer forum with senior management guest. Managing director or senior manager to chair a panel to field questions with the personnel manager.

3.00   Action planning session where delegates plan how and when they will implement target setting in their own departments. At this stage commitment will be made for local training in departments.

4.00   Course review to discuss feedback on the training course and for completion of course evaluation and debriefing documents.

4.30   Close

The two models presented above serve to illustrate that the approach to training will be determined in part by existing knowledge and skills as well as attitudes of managers. If there is likely to be a high level of resistance to target setting then the in-depth approach suggested by the two-day course will be more appropriate. Moving away from the workplace and giving more time to training is likely to open up objective discussion once managers have been able to air grievances and concerns through the catharsis which will probably occur on the first day. These issues will need to be heard and dealt with professionally. This will reduce the likelihood of accusations of the organization imposing the initiative on employees under duress.

Having provided training it is of vital importance to offer ongoing support to managers. It is frequently the case that we fall into the trap of assuming that because the managers have attended the training course they are sufficiently trained and confident to continue without further support. In fact it is not quite so simple: development extends beyond initial training and the skills of setting and reviewing targets will continue to be developed and refined with experience.

It is constructive to build on the real experience of setting targets and use such material to identify good practice and areas for continual development. Possible methods are for the training officer or personnel specialist to be sent copies of targets once they are set and to consider how well they meet the requirements of effective targets: are they specific, measurable, achievable and timebound? Including the human resource specialist on the circulation list for targets once they have been set enables records to be held and used for the purpose of, for example, training provision, succession planning and, not least of all, monitoring the effectiveness of the target setting initiative.

Methods of follow up might include one-to-one coaching or short, focused workshops. It is also a powerful technique to identify examples of good-quality targets and circulate sample copies in order to reinforce the success of target setting throughout the organization. Obviously it might be necessary to depersonalize such targets in order to preserve confidentiality.

HANDLING QUESTIONS DURING TRAINING

Inevitably if you are responsible for successful delivery of training on the subject of target setting you are likely to encounter a number of questions regarding how the initiative is going to work. Additionally, there are likely to be a number of questions about how to set targets in different functions. In Chapter 5 we gave you some examples of targets for different types of job role, ranging from the senior manager to the administrative job. It will be advantageous to be able to take such examples into a training session so that delegates can actually see what real targets might look like. It is even more powerful if you are able to produce targets that have been produced previously for real jobs in your organization.

One of the key barriers that you are likely to face is resistance to change if there has been no previous history of target setting in the organization. In many ways this is a natural human barrier that needs to be managed. It is helpful to consider the key stages we tend to pass through in the process of accepting change so that in providing the training or even through informal discussion you might guide employees through to the stage of acceptance. Figure 8.1 shows that often the first reaction to a new way of operating is to deny that it is relevant. At this stage you are likely to hear comments such as 'I do not need targets for my job – I have managed perfectly well in the past without them'. Interestingly, a good approach here is not to fight the denial in others but to accept that this is the first step towards ultimate acceptance. You would do well at this stage to accept that the other person has a right to a point of view, but talk from your experience or knowledge of other organizations or departments about their approach to target setting.

The next stage towards acceptance is antagonism: you are likely to hear comments such as 'You don't need targets for everything', 'This must just be flavour of the month', 'Surely there are more useful things you could be doing?'. Again, it is not necessarily the best approach to fight back directly. Stick to facts and provide examples of how it could work without being evangelical; this is more likely to help others move on to the next stage, which is mental try-out.

Mental try-out is where you hear comments such as 'I can see how it might work for the other department, but I'm not so sure I can see how it would work for me'. These words give away the fact that the person is attempting to visualize how target setting might work. At this stage there is a need to help them to picture what target setting might look like, such as providing relevant examples of successful target setting and how it could work here. Encourage real-life try-out without being over forceful; often a softer sell can be more powerful than relying on your authority or trying to force change.

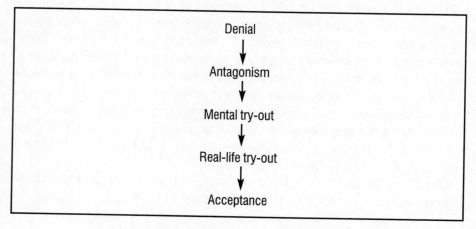

Figure 8.1 Stages in the process of change

Below there are ten questions that you are likely to encounter when delivering training and some suggestions regarding the sort of response to consider.

Questions	Suggested response
Why do we have to have targets for everything we do?	Clearly there is no need to have targets for everything. Some activities are just part of the job, but target setting ought to be about emphasizing the really important things and helping to move things forward, ultimately making an impact on the organization.
Surely setting targets will cramp creativity?	There is no intention to inhibit creativity. Indeed, targets can be set to encourage creative ideas and initiative.
I have managed in the past without having targets set, or for that matter without setting them for my staff and we have been successful. Why bother now?	Working to targets provides an opportunity to ensure the team is pulling in the same direction. It also ensures there are some clear measures of success defined and agreed from the start.
Surely there are some things you just can't measure?	Some things are more difficult to measure and some targets will be set where the measure is actually agreed through discussion rather than being able to provide a numerical measure.
Won't my staff feel threatened by me having targets set for them?	It may seem threatening at first, but it is important for them to see that they have a key role in determining and agreeing the targets themselves.
But what if I do not have the power to reward my staff for success against targets?	Whilst you may not have the say over salary increases, you may have discretion to provide intrinsic rewards such as opportunities for development and recognition.

Surely this is just the latest fad from the human resources department?	Target setting has become particularly popular in many organizations in recent years; however, the aim here is to get ideas from line managers regarding how the system would work. Do you have any recommendations?
I have heard it can be divisive setting targets from within the team. What do you think?	It can be divisive if team members are working against one another in a competitive sense; however, it can lend strength to a team if some common targets are set that all members of the team are working towards.
Isn't this a time-consuming exercise?	Obviously working through the process of target setting is time consuming but it does become easier the more used to this way of working you become. Consider time spent at the start setting targets as an investment because it means that the assessment process will be easier and much less time consuming.
I wouldn't know where to start in producing targets for my job. What do you suggest?	Try to identify the key things you would like to achieve in order to improve your contribution to the organization over the coming months. Also consider the skills that you would personally like to develop for the future.

Finally, in this chapter we provide some examples of handouts which could be provided in a training session as previously described.

Handout 1

TYPES OF TARGET

There should be a combination of types of target, weighted as the manager considers appropriate for the job/individual. The timescales of some targets may be only a few weeks or months if they relate to a specific project or task. At the other extreme some may cover the whole period if appropriate.

Organizational

Separate from the company's business target. It may be possible to identify a target that fits in with an organizational priority, eg relating to a customer relationship or implementation of the team briefing initiative.

Departmental

There will be particular issues that will help the efficiency/effectiveness of the department, eg relating to:

- improvement of interdepartmental communication;
- improvement of quality/speed of service to other departments;
- budgetary or cost control targets;
- recruitment or training.

Managerial

If the subordinate is a supervisor or manager it may be important to set some targets relating to this aspect of the job, eg:

- staff development;
- discipline/control of staff;
- recruitment/retention.

Technical

Development of technical skills or knowledge or achievement of technical tasks.

Individual

Targets should include at least one aimed at developing the individual. This could mean developing individual skills or improving a particular aspect of the individual's performance.

Handout 2

TARGET SETTING FOR DIFFERENT TYPES OF JOBS

Most managers could justifiably argue that it is difficult to set targets in their particular department or function. There are certain types of jobs where different approaches may be taken.

Managerial/supervisory

It may be possible to offer more supervisory responsibility than is currently being taken. Consider targets for appropriate aspects of the supervisory role, eg planning, supervision skill, administration, financial, communication.

Routine jobs and services

In some areas of the business the purpose is to provide a service or carry out predetermined tasks without a great deal of scope for discretion by the job holder in what to do or how to do it.

It may be possible to set a few core targets that apply to a number of people and then add a few individual targets with the intention of developing certain team members in a particular direction. If it is not possible to prepare the individual for career advancement it is still important to try to improve how well the job is being done.

In a service function it is always important to strive to improve the service to 'customers'. At more junior levels normally one target will relate to commitment to the job and flexibility.

Creative jobs

It is difficult to set targets that focus on creative aspects of a job because a certain amount of subjectivity prevails at the assessment stage. A key principle is not to set targets that cannot be assessed.

In all jobs certain *individual qualities* will be important and it is possible to set goals against these, eg:

- ability to work effectively with colleagues;
- self-presentation skills;
- relationships with other departments;
- ability to meet deadlines.

If it is important to set targets relating to the *creative* aspect of the job it is essential to agree at the outset how assessment will be made, eg:

- number of times ideas are rejected;
- how well a design is accepted by senior management;
- feedback from customers/clients.

Handout 3

CHECKLIST FOR SETTING EFFECTIVE TARGETS

Effective targets should:

- *Be measurable.* This could mean measurable in *quantifiable* terms. If this is not possible then discussion should take place and a record should be made of *standards expected.* There must be an understanding of what constitutes good/poor performance.
- *Include expected completion date or deadline* or agreement on what would be considered good/poor achievement in terms of timescale.
- *Focus on a maximum of six issues.* Identify areas of the job where achievement/improvement will have most impact. Balance organizational, departmental, managerial, technical and individual targets.
- *Be achievable but stretching.* 'Put a 5 foot 10 inch person into 6 feet 3 inches of water, and odds are he'll learn to swim. He may sputter and spit a bit, but he can always hop up off the bottom and get air. Put that same person in 7 feet 4 inches of water, and you may have a dead body on your hands' (Peters, 1989).
- *Be negotiated and agreed.* Manager and subordinate should prepare separately. Both meet to negotiate and agree targets.
- *Be subject to mid-term modification* by agreement, if external circumstances/conditions change. This does not mean modification of targets should become normal practice. If, however, changes in circumstances are out of the individual's control there could be a case for modification.
- *Entail a two-way commitment.* The manager is committing to assist and provide the necessary resources for targets to be achieved. The subordinate is committing to work towards the targets.

Handout 4

METHODS OF MEASUREMENT AND ASSESSMENT

- Cost
- Speed/deadlines
- Accuracy/number of mistakes
- Evidence of achievement of a task
- Knowledge
- Skill level
- Examples of behaviour change
- Amount of supervision needed

ACTIVITY

Consider the implementation of target setting in your own organization.

- Who should and could be invited in as a senior management representative to support the initiative?
- In what way could such representatives be used to help in a training course?
- What methods and type of training would you consider appropriate for your organization?

Part IV

Goal Achievement

9

Unlocking Human Potential

SUMMARY

In this chapter we move on to look at the subject of how to increase the chances of success in achieving personal goals. Many of the findings here are drawn from our recent research into the achievement of human potential. In particular we:

- explain the background to our research into the subject of the achievement of human potential;
- propose a model of human behaviour that shows how we develop our own self-concept;
- consider how we develop a self-concept and discuss the influence of 'experts' on our lives;
- Discuss ways of achieving personal goals including the use of flooding and desensitization; and
- Introduce the concepts of visualization, imagery and self-assertion statements, which are then explained in detail in Chapter 10.

This discussion on achieving success by harnessing the power of our own minds is drawn from three key sources. First, we have conducted research with successful chief executives regarding their approach to achieving success in a personal and business sense. This has provided us with a powerful insight into both the practical and the cognitive, or thinking, techniques that these people use in order to achieve success. Interestingly, many of the anecdotal findings on the achievement of human potential in the sporting arena are applied either consciously or intuitively by successful people in organizations.

Secondly, we have been delivering an international executive development programme that focuses on the achievement of personal goals through bringing about lasting changes in behaviour. We have developed this programme to include the models and techniques discussed here. Furthermore, we have monitored the success of those executives who have combined cognitive techniques with physical skills and have identified that this approach is significantly more likely to bring about real change than focusing on skills alone.

Finally, drawing on our material in *The Power of Personal Influence* (Hale and Whitlam, 1995), we focus particularly on how you can apply practical techniques in order to increase the likelihood of goal achievement.

A MODEL FOR UNDERSTANDING BEHAVIOUR

In Figure 9.1 we propose a model of human behaviour that explores the importance of our thinking on our own self image. Working through this model will demonstrate the processes we all use either subconsciously, or indeed consciously, and we will then look at how knowledge of such a model can provide valuable insight into how to manage our own thought processes in order to move towards the achievement of personal goals.

This model suggests that we are continuously behaving: whether talking, reading, walking or doing anything else, we can describe any of our waking actions as behaviour. Additionally, subsequent to any behaviour we

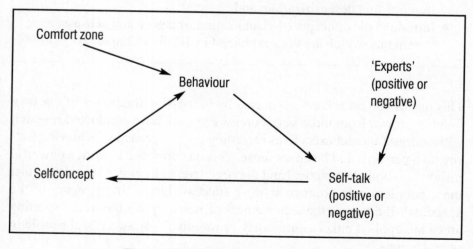

Figure 9.1 A model of human behaviour

are continuously reviewing our performance. Sometimes this review or evaluation is conscious and sometimes it is less so. The way we review is often described as 'self-talk'; in other words, we will have conversations with ourselves in our head. This is not abnormal, consider for a moment how you think: the chances are you are regularly saying to yourself things like 'This is going well' or 'I am not doing too well here'. (Interestingly, studies into mental illness suggest that sometimes individuals are not able to recognize their self-talk as their own; in other words, they will attribute the 'voices' they hear to someone else.)

We all engage in self-talk; unfortunately, however, this self-talk is usually negative in nature. So we will often review ourselves in a negative light, which is not helped by the fact that our thinking is strongly influenced by certain other people who we will describe as 'experts'. These are not necessarily true experts but anyone we allow to influence our thinking about ourselves. Again, our research has shown that we are more often influenced by negative experts than positive ones. An 'expert' might be defined as anyone we permit to influence our thinking. In early life these people may include parents, peers or friends; in later life they may be spouses, bosses, colleagues, or indeed, anyone who we believe has more experience or knowledge than ourselves.

The important thing in this notion of 'expert' is that it is only necessary for us to believe that the person has more knowledge than ourselves, rather than have proof of the actual existence of such knowledge. Unfortunately for most of us, we have probably had many experiences of 'experts' who have provided a negative rather than a positive influence in our lives. If over time these beliefs are reinforced, ultimately the individual develops a clear picture of themselves in this negative light. Certainly some of these beliefs are inappropriate; they have their basis not in the truth, but in our own and other people's interpretations. But effectively, this is how self belief is developed.

Take, for instance, the example of the small child who comes home from kindergarten having spent the day painting a picture. In fact, for a 4-year-old the picture is of a usual standard and the parents, being quite sensitive, will make comments such as 'Oh how nice! Tell me what it is.' The child describes the picture in some detail and receives some encouraging parental comments. Then the child's older brother comes home from school and the child runs up to her older brother proudly showing her painting. The big brother takes one look at it and, being less sensitive in giving feedback than the parents, says 'That's rubbish, that is. Everyone knows that trees aren't blue . . . and everyone knows that you're supposed to paint inside the lines'. Now the younger child does not know words like 'expert' but you can almost hear her self-talk as she walks off sadly: 'I am not much good at painting – I know this because my brother, who is an expert, told me so'. What is interesting here is that the perceived expert is the sibling and not so much the parent. Of course the brother is seen as expert because he has his art exhibited on the refrigerator; furthermore, friends and relatives are taken into the kitchen to view it!

The power of such 'experts' in our lives cannot be underestimated. What is important is to recognize who are and who have been the 'experts', ie any people we allow to affect our thinking about ourselves. We should particularly question who the negative 'experts' are and the validity of their expertise. The exercise at the end of Chapter 10 is designed to help you to reflect on such questions.

So we behave, we review our performance and engage in self-talk, and we are influenced by so-called 'experts'. All this leads to the dominant picture we have of ourselves: our 'self-concept'. One way of looking at our self-concept is that it is the sum total of everything that has happened to us and our evaluation of it. Self-concept clearly comprises attitudes, beliefs, experiences and values (see Figure 9.2).

What is significant in terms of the achievement of goals, is that we tend to act in accordance with our self-concept. To operate outside of our self-concept is to move outside of our 'comfort-zone', and this makes us very

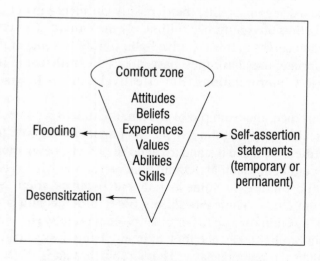

Figure 9.2 Expanding the comfort zone

uneasy. The comfort zone is the sum collection of the attitudes, habits, values and beliefs that make up my self-image: that is to say the picture that I hold in my head of who I am. This self-image then acts in a way to control my behaviour, as generally I act in accordance with my self-image, or the way I know or believe that I should act. Thus when I behave in a way that I know and believe I am, I am relatively comfortable. Behaving in a way that is inconsistent with my self-image is likely to result in stress or discomfort. So if one aspect of my self-concept says that I am not the sort of person who is good at public speaking and I am asked if I could make a formal presentation regarding an area of my expertise, then my reaction is likely to be to try to avoid it. Just the thought of making the presentation will cause a physical reaction; a faster heart beat and a shot of adrenaline.

There have been two classic approaches to developing human potential by expanding the comfort zone. One is through the use of 'flooding'. Flooding works in the following way. If you have a particular fear, take for instance the example above, a fear of making presentations, and you are forced into making a major presentation in front of a massive audience, one of two things will happen: either you will have a positive experience, the presentation will be an overwhelming success and you will be cured of your fear; or you will have a profoundly damaging experience that serves to reinforce your previously held self-belief. Such flooding is used in many organizations, and for many individuals it is a useful and expedient approach – they swim. Unfortunately, some people are not so lucky – they drown! Consequently, where flooding has been used unsuccessfully, the impact on the individual is highly stressful, but it can also be catastrophic: the person may not try anything like it ever again. And for every person who survives the experience, there are several who drown. So flooding as a means of helping you to broaden your comfort zone in order to achieve personal goals is clearly a high-risk strategy.

The second method of broadening one's comfort zone is known as desensitization. This works on the basis of moving the individual outside of their comfort zone in a step-by-step, gradual way. So in order to become increasingly comfortable with the concept of making presentations, one would work through the following steps over a period of months.

- Sit in on someone else's presentation and make notes.
- Help the other person prepare their presentation.
- Contribute to part of a presentation led by the other person.
- Lead a presentation with support from someone else.
- Make a presentation alone.

This is a type of coaching, and you might consider this approach in terms of both your own development and in developing others. Of course, it is more time consuming than using flooding, but it is a much safer approach.

One thing that flooding techniques and desensitization have in common is that they both focus on changing behaviour before making internal changes in one's thinking. While this may seem normal, it is worth reflecting on the question 'What comes first our thoughts or our deeds?'. In psychology it is commonly accepted that a model of behaviour is:

Thinking affects
Feeling which affects
Behaviour.

Indeed, in some areas of behavioural counselling delinquent children, for instance, are taught to address their emotions, feelings and thoughts as a prerequisite to tackling issues of behaviour. In a similar way we found that successful individuals have a tendency to consciously address the issue of their thinking as something just as important as addressing their behavioural skills in order to achieve their personal goals. This led us to experiment with use of self-assertion statements and we have discovered that it is possible to significantly increase an individual's comfort zone, in other words, unlock human potential by such methods. Self-assertion statements are statements we make for our own use, which adhere to certain rules, and which help us to see ourselves having achieved success. We explain how to write and imprint self-assertion statements in the next chapter. Self-assertion statements are a way of ensuring our self-talk or inner dialogues are positive. They are also a way of programming our subconscious so that we take control of our own thoughts, which will in turn make an impact on our behaviour.

CHARACTERISTICS OF HIGH ACHIEVERS

When we studied the characteristics of people who were extremely successful in achieving their personal goals, whether work goals or personal ones, we found the following. High achievers tended to have significant similarities:

- Heightened awareness of the impact of other people on their inner dialogues, particularly the negative impact.
- Regularly engaging in the use of imagery, and an ability to experience actual feelings and see detail when fantasizing or using imagery.

- Frequently using 'internal coaching' to improve performance.
- A tendency to encourage themselves either before, during or after doing something, particularly in threatening or potentially difficult situations.
- Recognition of the potential impact of negative thoughts and how vulnerable they could be if such thoughts were not managed.
- The regular use of repetitive imagery of success to create or visualize how things might be in the future.
- The ability to visualize broad pictures but with the capability of homing in on fine details.

Our findings are supported by some of the research into the achievement of human potential in the sporting world, where it has been known for some time that mental practice and visualization can improve physical performance. As long ago as 1965 experiments in examining methods of gymnastic coaching discovered that it was possible for people to learn gymnastic skills simply by reading a mechanical analysis of the skills combined with mentally practising. What was particularly interesting in these results was that this approach applied even when the learner had no previous experience of the skill.

Other more anecdotal examples include the recollections of the golfer Jack Nicklaus who in his book *Golf My Way* describes how he would use imagery before every golf shot in order to visualize success. Similarly, in the clinical field, work with stutterers highlighted the fact that stutterers held a stronger self-image of themselves as stutterers than non-stutterers and because of this they felt more comfortable relating to the world as stutterers. It was shown that with mental practice and visualization techniques the problem could be significantly alleviated. In the medical context there is a growing body of evidence to indicate the effectiveness of imagery in treating a whole spectrum of conditions ranging from depression to chronic pain.

People with strong visualization capabilities tended to have the following types of experience:

- extensive vivid fantasies
- hallucinatory fantasies
- pretending to be someone else
- sensory motor experiences
- vivid personal memories
- telepathy and other psychic experiences
- out-of-body experiences
- automatic writing

- religious visions
- healing
- apparitions.

At least 53 per cent of the high achieving individuals who took part in our research stated that they had experienced one or more of the above phenomena at some point in their life.

We asked those with strong powers of visualization whether their use of imagery is linked to any context or particular time of day. The majority said their strongest visualization experiences were when they were relaxed or semi-conscious, and were particularly vivid when in a state of limbo between wakefulness and sleeping in the morning or last thing at night. This is sometimes referred to as the 'alpha state', when the body is relaxed and the mind is still working, but with a slow down in brainwaves.

Many chief executives we interviewed related that in order to prepare themselves for big events such as board meetings or important presentations, they would rehearse mentally by addressing the particularly difficult aspects and visualizing a successful outcome; so they would actually see themselves concluding the meeting successfully, whether this meant gaining agreement from the shareholders or receiving applause from the audience of the presentation.

There are some parallels here with the approach to mental preparation taken by top athletes and sports people. Linford Christie, winner of the gold medal for the 100-metres sprint in the 1993 world championships, was interviewed after the event. He was shown a replay of himself seconds before the start, where he was standing absolutely still with his eyes shut. When asked what he was doing at that moment he explained that he was running (and winning) the race in his head. He further explained that he had done this hundreds of times before, and every time he had always crossed the finish line first.

We have known for some time that mental practice does actually improve physical performance, yet up until now the use of such techniques appears to have been in the domain of the sports person. Our research not only confirms the original findings but demonstrates that these techniques are widely used by other successful individuals across a variety of situations and circumstances. Clearly such mental processes can be learned as a skill and can be developed to assist us in achieving personal goals.

We asked some of the most successful chief executive officers and senior management of major international organizations to explain how they built their own confidence to ensure that, in business situations, they are likely to be successful. Our research revealed that there are some common techniques and methods, which appear to be used quite naturally by these successful managers, and which contribute significantly to their success.

We have categorized the approaches into a number of specific techniques. When introducing these techniques on skills development programmes, we found that they helped managers significantly to increase their chances of success and develop skills resulting in lasting changes in behaviour. In the next chapter we address the subject of the achievement of goals in a very practical way by explaining how to use these techniques.

ACTIVITY

Work through the exercise at the end of Chapter 10 and reflect on you own self-concept and the extent to which you have been influenced by positive and negative 'experts'. Reappraise whether you should continue to view the negative ones as experts. Consider the nature of your self-talk and assess the extent to which it is positive or negative. Finally, use the action planning part of the exercise to identify ways in which you would like to address your thinking patterns.

Consider the same issues with respect to individuals you have influence over. Think about situations and relationships where you may be perceived as an 'expert' and consider the impact you may have on others regarding their self-concept.

10

Techniques of Goal Achievement

SUMMARY

This chapter takes a practical look at the key techniques that we have identified as assisting the individual to achieve personal goals. These will be of relevance to anyone working towards achievement of their own goals, as well as the manager who wishes to coach subordinates and help them to realize their potential. In particular we look at:

- the use of visualization and imagery to help create pictures of success;
- the process by which images are imprinted in our minds;
- the application of vision building in teams;
- how to write effective self-assertion statements.

The last chapter discussed the importance of taking control of our thought processes to unlock our human potential; a necessary precursor to using some of the techniques associated with goal achievement is to unblock our thinking and to ensure our self-perception is not unduly affected by distorting factors. This means controlling who we allow to influence our thinking about us, that is the so-called 'experts'. We can now explore the specific cognitive skills associated with goal achievement. First, we look at the use of imagery.

PREPARING FOR THE ONE-OFF: USING SELF-TALK AND VISUALIZATION

Our ability to visualize or picture success is more than simply 'positive thinking'. If we can manage the pictures we carry in our heads of ourselves or of situations, and if we can control the internal conversations we have, our perception will become heightened and we are more likely to see the things that we want. Seeing these things is the prerequisite to taking action. We are moved into action by the repeated use of this imagery, but more repetition produces lasting and sustained change.

To demonstrate the power of these principles, try the following simple experiment. The next time you are driving and are worried that you will not be able to find a parking space, instead of waiting until you arrive in the town centre and then getting into a cycle of negative self-talk, about the lack of parking spaces, spend about a minute before you leave home thinking along the following lines.

- Visualize the town centre, particularly in the area that you would like to park. Try to see as much detail as possible.
- Picture where the cars are usually parked.
- Imagine yourself reversing into a space somewhere in the general area.
- Imagine the feeling of relief at finding a place so soon.

As a result of undertaking the above you may be surprised at how quickly you find a parking space. This is primarily caused by your perception being heightened: you are seeing things that were always there, whereas normally you would wait until you had arrived before you start 'looking', and would have missed numerous parking opportunities.

Using this visualization, you will find that when you get to within 800m of the area you had been visualizing, you will suddenly start seeing all the opportunities for parking, such as:

- people reaching in their pockets for their car keys;
- exhaust pipes starting up;
- doors opening;
- people walking determinedly towards vehicles.

In effect, with this technique you are first visualizing success and then utilizing the way in which perception works to spot opportunities that abound. Of course, you can use this technique in many situations: you might think of, for instance, making a presentation, chairing a meeting, playing a sport or attending an interview.

What we are describing here is the temporary use of visualization, whereby the individual, in order to achieve success in a temporary or one-off situation, harnesses the power of his or her cognitive processes. We found when interviewing high achievers that they appear to possess strong imaginative skills including the ability to picture or visualize situations, but visualization and imagery are skills that can be developed and refined.

A chief executive of an international petro-chemical company described sitting down before a shareholders' meeting and using visualization to picture a successful result. Such an outcome might include seeing and hearing the meeting clapping him, or alternatively seeing smiling faces. Another executive from an international brewing company stated that she would usually make herself relax using imagery prior to doing something difficult, such as informing staff of major restructure or redeployment. In such circumstances she recognized the importance of being able to visualize herself succeeding in her goal of communicating effectively.

An international business professor explained that he had recognized the link between his thinking prior to starting an assignment and the eventual outcome. In particular, he found that where he was able to visualize people wanting his help, or where he saw himself as being made welcome and quickly encouraged to contribute, he found that the outcome was infinitely more favourable. By contrast, the opposite was also true. If there was a tendency to think in advance that an event was likely to fail, this would seem to serve as a self-fulfilling prophecy and failure would indeed be the result.

When running major training programmes we have also experimented with the notion of temporary visualization. On some programmes we have found our self-talk running along the lines of: 'This is a tough group, they're going to be hard work and are unlikely to be interested', 'It's Friday, they're going to be thinking about going home; in fact, we are thinking about going home', 'There is bound to be one awkward one who argues with everything', etc. We referred to this as self-talk; however, we found ourselves sharing these thoughts with colleagues, so the message was reinforced through conversation and given legitimacy through the acknowledgement of others. Not surprisingly, after such preparatory conversations, more often than not, in practice the outcome was negative. Taking exactly the same training programmes, we then consciously changed the nature of our self-talk with remarkable effects. We said things such as: 'This is going to be a good experience. We know the material well and we know that it works', 'we are getting better all the time at presenting this programme', 'the group is likely to be interesting and fun to work with', and 'just as we have something to offer we are sure we can learn something valuable from them'. The impact of simply changing our self-talk was significant; it was as though we had reversed the negative self-fulfilling prophecy and used the same phenomenon in a positive way. When we combined the use of positive self-talk with visualization the impact was enhanced even further. So we would picture the people even before we had met them and we would visualize the exercises and discussions we would become engaged in. We would work at seeing interested and smiling faces and delegates who were asking plenty of questions.

So using visualization combined with temporary self-assertion statements is a powerful way of preparing for the achievement of one-off or occasional goals. The techniques are similar to the more permanent self-assertion statements described below, the primary difference is that they are not written down, nor are they necessarily repeated. Positive self-talk and visualization appears to be of particular value when there is little time to prepare. But they are also useful in supporting progress towards other more formal permanent goals; and it is in these circumstances that many successful sports people use the technique.

TEAM TALK AND VISION BUILDING

As well as using the powers of visualization and self-talk for individuals we have found that there is much to be gained by using similar techniques when working with teams. Again, much can be learned from looking at the approach taken by successful 'super teams' in the sporting field. They will tend to put a great deal of emphasis on talking themselves up rather than down in anticipation of important competitions. This often entails positive 'team talk', to ensure the team is psychologically focused on their goal and that all the members of the team are equally prepared mentally. Indeed, many teams will mention that they are well 'psyched-up' prior to a major game. Conversely, unsuccessful teams will allow their team talk to degenerate and they will paint pictures of failure that becomes self-fulfilling.

In a business context there is a trend towards operating in team environments and in particular towards multidisciplinary teams. Increasingly teams are having to operate across international boundaries, often without the facility for being together all the time. There is also recognition in many organizations of the importance of allowing teams to evolve, change shape and disband when they have completed their primary objective.

All this suggests even more need for clarity of focus in terms of both business objectives or vision and the goals of the individual. Let's look first at how visualization can help to clarify long-term objectives of organizations. Many are spending time drawing up vision or mission statements to help provide direction for the organization. All too often this has been seen as the preserve of the top team, but it is equally important for functional and project teams to go through a vision-building process. In the worst examples of vision building one or two people on the team will attempt to define the vision for the future without involving all the team members and the vision will then be published in elegant words for all to read. Equally inadequate is when people in the organization are asked about their team's vision and say that they know there is one but they are not sure what it says. In the most successful organizational teams the process of defining a vision is seen as a way of ensuring that all team members have bought into the same overall goals. This is not to say that individuals will not have their own personal goals, but these are not likely to conflict with the goals of the team as a whole. Think, for instance, of the successful sports team where there is a clear overarching goal such as to be top of the league. This does not stop individuals having their own goals, such as to contribute more to the team, to gain promotion to the next team up, or to secure their place for the future.

Building a team vision is like scattering iron filings on the table top and then stroking the table underneath with a magnet. The iron filings do two things: they move closer together and they line up so they are pointing in the same direction. In the same way, building a team vision can be a powerful bonding experience.

Team vision building is a way of capturing the benefits of visualization by asking the team to consider and define what success looks like for them. We would recommend the following approach. First the individuals should be asked to think ahead to the future and picture successful team achievement. They should commit their thoughts to writing against some structure. This might take the form of:

'We want to ...   (statement of overall objective or why the team exists)
which ...   (qualifies the objective)
in order to ...   (a statement of the outcomes required)
as measured by ...   (how the team will know when it has been successful).

Once each member has been through this exercise there should be a discussion to define the team vision statement. This will naturally be a difficult and often lengthy discussion, but the important thing here is that the members are buying into a common vision of what success looks like. The key point is that the process of working through the vision-building exercise as a team is just as important as the output or content that results. Each word should be chosen with care and each member of the team should be committed to the words chosen.

Following the guidelines shown above one organization we have worked with produced a vision statement as follows:

'*We want to* provide a high quality international advertising consultancy,
which is of mutual benefit to the business and our client,
in order to maximize profits,
as measured by increased market share and repeat business.'

This short statement emphasizes a number of key issues, such as the importance of the concept of partnership and the significance of building long-term client relationships. Clearly this sort of vision statement lends itself to a strategic or senior level team, but it is equally appropriate to build vision statements in teams down through the organization. The vision is strengthened if it includes words that conjure up pictures, images or emotions associated with success. Hence one creative team in the above advertising consultancy developed a vision that said:

'*We want to* create innovative advertising solutions,
which meet the needs of key clients and stimulate team members,
in order to contribute to the goals of the business,
as measured by internal and external acclaim.'

This incorporates the aims of creating and being innovative as well as how the team should be seen both within the organization and from the outside. Successful teams are strong in their ability to build relationships with other teams and 'sponsors' rather than putting up barriers, and this is reflected in the vision statement of the above team.

So vision building drawing on the powers of visualization and positive team talk is an approach that lends itself to focusing teams on the successful achievement of their goals. As well as formulating an overall longer-term vision that really encapsulates the team's *raison d'être* it is possible to use the same process to develop short-term goals and objectives.

USING SELF-ASSERTION STATEMENTS

The other approach that we have found to be powerful in helping managers move towards the achievement of their goals entails the use of self-assertion statements. Self-assertion statements define the goal that the individual is working towards, but they also draw on visualization. Images of success are imprinted on the subconscious and ultimately these create a dominant picture of goal achievement. This results in a new belief, and ultimately behaviour will move in line with thinking, leading to actual achievement of the goal.

Self-assertion statements can be temporary or permanent; repetition can help achieve lasting and sustained change in behaviour. Our research in this area has shown that in trying to bring about lasting changes in behaviour following skills development, the chances of success are increased three-fold if self-assertion statements are used in conjunction with practical techniques.

Self-assertion statements are simply statements of desired outcomes or behaviours that are written down and then imprinted on the mind. They accelerate the process of moving towards the achievement of personal goals and objectives by taking the time to imprint only images that we want onto our subconscious minds, rather than other less helpful messages. Self-assertion statements are about establishing new beliefs and counteracting old beliefs about ourselves by effectively programming our subconscious. This programming is a normal and natural process; however, by using self-assertion statements we are taking control of the process, rather than leaving things to chance.

The technique follows three critical steps.

1 Identify and define the desired change, ie, recognize what needs changing.
2 Draft the self-assertion statement (making sure that it subscribes to the principles described below) and ensuring that it specifies a successful outcome.
3 Imprint by reading the self-assertion statement at least twice a day, and by imagining yourself as a person with the changed behaviour. The reinforcement of repetition combined with the visualization will produce a powerful change in your self-concept and subsequently your behaviour. (The imprinting should be done night and morning for at least 20 days.)

Self-assertion statements work by initially creating discomfort with our self-image, or how we see ourselves. This discomfort increases the more we imprint the new images. Eventually, by repetition we start to create a new dominant picture of reality as well as adding to the level of discomfort. Slowly we start to change our behaviour to match the new image or dominant picture of ourselves, consequently we begin to actually act in accordance with the new picture or belief.

There are a number of guidelines to follow in writing self-assertion statements.

1 Make the statement personal

You can only affirm for yourself. Do not try to affirm qualities or changes in other people or to correct or alter situations you cannot control. In writing your self-assertion statements, you are changing your self-image, or how you see yourself. Only you can deliberately control the input of information and the visualization that brings about the change of your subconscious self-image. Therefore, in most cases, your self-assertion statement will start with the word 'I'.

2 Use positive language
Only write out your self-assertion statements in a positive way. Do not describe what you are trying to move away from or eliminate. You must vividly paint the picture of success for your subconscious in a positive statement. For example, do not make a statement like 'I am no longer poor at contributing to meetings', but make a positive statement like 'I have a useful and interesting contribution to make in team meetings'. The secret is to write a statement that enables you to picture completely the change you desire.

3 Use the present tense
Write your self-assertion statements in the present tense. The reason we only use the present tense in describing our statement is that this is the only time-frame the subconscious operates in. Phrases like 'some day', 'maybe' and 'tomorrow' will create pictures that make you feel detached from the behavioural change you want to experience now. You want to feel as though the change is already happening and that you are experiencing the change inside your own mind and body.

4 Avoid comparisons
Self-asserting is a personal process. You are a unique person and if you attempt to compare yourself with others, you will have no way of measuring your personal progress. You may become discouraged by not measuring up to others, or you may get false clues as to the change in your self-image by being better than someone who is less capable. Do not assert that you are 'as good as' or 'better than' anyone else. Just strive to bring about the changes in your self-image that you desire by asserting the qualities that are best for you.

5 Use visual images
Describe the activity you are asserting in terms that create pictures of you performing in an easy and anxiety free manner. Your subconscious actions should be described by statements that start with 'I easily', 'I quickly', 'I enjoy', 'I love to', 'I thrive on' and 'I show'. Statements like these carry a picture of action and accomplishment that does not cause you to feel either threatened or pushed. The result is that you keep moving towards success with confidence.

Do not indicate just the ability 'I can', in your self-assertion statements because this will not produce change. You already have that ability. What you must indicate strongly is actual achievement. Statements like 'I am' and 'I have' clearly express to the subconscious the picture of the behavioural change that you desire. By using self-assertion statements you are assuming on the subconscious level that you are already acting like the person you indicate you want to become. The more you subconsciously act as if you are already in possession of that quality, the faster your self-image will make it evident in your daily actions. By seeing success you also help eliminate some of the stress usually associated with trying to achieve a goal.

6 Use powerful words

Try to put as much power and excitement in the wording of your self-assertion statements as you can by vividly stating your behaviour in colourful terms. Words that spark an emotional picture in your subconscious help to make the experience in your assertion more believable and attractive. Write your self-assertion statements to create feelings such as enjoyment, pride, happiness and accomplishment. Incidentally, the more emotion the faster the change. Some examples of starting phrases include: 'I warmly', 'I happily' and 'I enthusiastically'.

7 Be realistic

It is important for you to assert only as much as you can honestly imagine yourself becoming or performing. The basic rule is do not overshoot or undershoot. Try to have such a clear and vivid picture of the end result you want to accomplish that you accurately stay on course with your goal. Do not try to assert perfection. It is generally self-defeating to make assumptions about yourself or your accomplishments that you know have very little chance of ever happening or lasting. By using terms like 'I always', 'every time I', or 'I'll never' you can place unrealistic demands on yourself.

Clearly if you were to set a self-assertion statement that said 'I enjoy the feeling of winning the London marathon' then simply reading the statement and waiting for the victory will lead to disappointment. It is important to combine physical training with the psychological technique. It is worth noting, however, that top athletes who are often very close to their rivals in terms of physical ability, will use psychological techniques such as self-assertion statements and visualization to give them the physical edge over the competition.

Finally, you should remember that your personal self-assertion statements should be for yourself only, because people may constantly try to remind you of the 'old' self-image. Without really meaning to hold you back, the people around you may get upset when you start changing. If we reveal our personal goals and self-assertion statements to others, it allows them to work against us and very often causes us to fail to accomplish our goals. Use good judgement, only reveal your self-assertion statements to those people who need to know them and who can help you to realize them more quickly.

A number of examples of self-assertion statements which are categorized into management, team and personal areas are shown in Figure 10.1 below.

Management Self-assertion Statements

I am an expert at delegating responsibilities and seeing our people experience the achievement of results.

I always find the satisfaction that comes from developing my people extremely rewarding.

I enjoy the results that come from positive thinking.

I consistently receive tremendous gratification from 100 per cent customer satisfaction.

Team Self-assertion Statements

We treat all our customers like they were our only customer and the effect is that people come back to us, which really gives us a buzz.

We are true professionals in our approach to all our job activities and we like the feeling of respect this generates.

We pride ourselves on our company image in the community.

We easily keep our records up to date so that information can be quickly found.

Personal Self-assertion Statements

I like and respect myself. I know I am a worthy, capable and valuable person.

I enjoy my life, my profession and my relationships with other people and have a good balanced lifestyle.

I show others that I'm a person who does not give things up easily.

I have had many successful experiences using self-assertion statements and I take temporary setbacks easily.

Figure 10.1 Examples of Self-assertion Statements

IMPRINTING SELF-ASSERTION STATEMENTS

It is critical to continue to imprint your self-assertion statements once you have written them and we would recommend the following approach.

Reading

Read the words of your self-assertion statements as many times as you can each day, this provides a consistent trigger resulting in reinforcement The best times to read and imprint your self-assertion statements are generally early in the morning, soon after you wake and just before you go to sleep. Alternatively, you can read them at any time during your day, ideally when you are relaxed and have the available time. Repetition of the self-assertion statement is essential.

Imaging

As you read your self-assertion statements you should be trying to vividly picture yourself clearly having accomplished the change you want or the success you intend to achieve. You are displacing old self-images with new pictures of how you want to feel and act. Remember you are practising and experiencing the change consciously to begin with, but through your imaging you are recording your images into your mind. Very quickly you will find yourself moving easily and naturally to the newly imagined levels of performance.

Feelings

Feeling the emotion you want is very important for imprinting. Gather up the feelings that you know will accompany the accomplished goal and enjoy them each time you imprint your self-assertion. The assertion will affect your system in a positive way in direct proportion to the frequency you use vividness of imagery and emotional involvement.

Generally speaking, the impact of imprinting your self-assertion can be broken down as follows.

Reading	10% impact
Reading and picturing	55% impact
Reading, picturing and feeling	100% impact

Importantly, when using self-assertion statements it is essential to realize that you should not try to force a change in your behaviour. Keep reading the self-assertion statements, keep imprinting, but do not initially do any-thing different. If such change is forced, then it will be 'white knuckle change' – the result of this stress is that you will be unlikely to continue with the change.

Eventually, when the time is right, that is to say when you have repro-grammed your beliefs and established a new dominant picture of reality, then the necessary change will just happen naturally. What we are describ-ing here is change that starts within us, and works its way outside into our behaviour.

EXERCISE: MANAGING INTERNAL CHANGE

Purpose

To enable you to explore and understand a number of issues related to the subject of thought processes and to identify ways in which such processes can be improved.

Instructions

Consider the following six key questions about how you think. Use the completed exercise to consider any changes you wish to bring about in your thinking.

1 How much of my self-talk is positive?

-5	-4	-3	-2	-1	+1	+2	+3	+4	+5

Negative   Positive

What is my evidence for this rating?

2 Who have been, or who are the significant 'experts' in my life?

	Positive	Negative
1		
2		
3		
4		
5		

3 (a) What general beliefs do I hold about myself?

Positive	Negative

3(b) How or where did I learn these beliefs?

Positive	Negative

4 Specific beliefs related to goal achievement

	Strongly disagree			Strongly agree
(a) I always prepare mentally for major events.	1	2	3	4
(b) I always evaluate my performance in a balanced way.	1	2	3	4
(c) I try to give myself a positive experience after a disappointing setback.	1	2	3	4
(d) I am conscious of who I allow to influence my thinking about me.	1	2	3	4
(e) I use visualization and imagery to give myself a picture of success.	1	2	3	4
(f) I keep a list of personal goals and targets.	1	2	3	4
(g) I regularly think about success and picture how I am moving towards it.	1	2	3	4

5 How clearly do I see things?

1	2	3	4	5	6	7	8	9	10

Always
distorting
events

Very
clearly

6 How badly do I want to change?

1	2	3	4	5	6	7	8	9	10

Not committed   Highly committed

Action plan

ACTIVITY

Consider one of your personal goals and draw up a self-assertion statement using the guidelines above to ensure that you adhere to the key principles. Commit the statement to writing and keep it in a place where you can readily access it in the early morning and late evening. If you persist with this approach you should start to see tangible results within 21 days. Ensure you read the self-assertion statement at least twice a day and use imagery to visualize success.

References

Alder, H (1991) 'Seeing is believing: the natural way to success', *Management Decision*, 29(1).

Boyatsis (1982) *The Competent Manager*, Wiley, New York (1990).

Department of Trade and Industry (1992) *The Case for Costing Quality*, DTI, London.

Gallwey, W T (1986a) *The Inner Game of Golf*, Pan, London.

Gallwey, W T (1986b) *The Inner Game of Tennis*, Pan, London.

Garratt, B (1990) *Creating a Learning Organization: a Guide to Leadership, Learning and Development*, Director Books in association with the Institute of Directors, Cambridge.

Hale, R and Whitlam, P (1998) *Powering up Performance Management*, Gower.

Hale, R and Whitlam, P (1997) *Practical Problem Solving and Decision Making*, Kogan Page, London

Hale, R and Whitlam, P (1995) *The Power of Personal Influence*, McGraw-Hill, Maidenhead.

Hale, R and Whitlam, P (1997) *Towards the Virtual Organisation*, McGraw-Hill, Maidenhead.

Higgs, M and Rowland, D (1992) 'All Pigs are Equal?', Management Education & Development, Vol 23, Part 4, p349–362

Handy, C (1981) *Understanding Organizations*, Penguin, Harmondsworth.

Institute of Personnel Management (1992) *Performance Management in the UK, An Analysis of the Issues*, IPM, London.

Kane, J S and Freeman, K A (1986) 'MBO and performance appraisal: a mixture that's not a solution, part 1', *Personnel*, December.

Kane, J S and Freeman, K A (1987) 'MBO and performance appraisal: a mixture that's not a solution, part 2', *Personnel*, February.

Katzenbach, J R and Smith, D K (1993) *The Wisdom of Teams*, Harvard Business School Press, Boston.

Locke, E and Latham, G (1990) *A Theory of Goal Setting and Task Performance*, Prentice Hall, New York.

Lowe, P (1993) *Performance Appraisal*, Kogan Page, London.

McCallum, C (1993) *How to Design and Introduce Appraisal Training*, Kogan Page, London.

Maltz, M (1986) *Psycho-cybernetics*, Simon & Schuster, New York.

Management Charter Initiative (1991) *Crediting Competence, A Guide to APL for Practising Managers*, MCI, London.

Nicklaus, J (1976) *Golf My Way*, Penguin, Harmondsworth.

Peters, T (1989) *Thriving on Chaos*, Pan in association with Macmillan, London.

Peters, T and Waterman, R (1982) *In Search of Excellence*, Harper & Row, New York.

Rodgers, R and Hunter, J E (1991) 'Impact of management by objectives on organizational productivity', *Journal of Applied Psychology*, April.

Shone, R (1984) *Creative Visualisation*, Thorsons.

Whitlam, Peter J (1993) 'Imagery: its application to goal achievement', paper presented at the International Training and Development Conference, Brussels, and held by IMC Buckingham, England.

VIDEOS AND CD-ROM RESOURCES

BBC for Business (+44 (0) 181 576 2000)

'Coaching for Results' (Video): Video based training resource based on skills of coaching using drama, documentary interviews and a real life coaching session.

'Coaching the Team' (Video): Case studies of US-based Steelcase and the Royal Marines showing how they have developed teams.

'The Empowering Appraisal' (Video): Target review and objective setting from an organizational and individual perspective.

Fenman Training (+44 (0) 1353 665 533)

'Feedback Techniques' (Video): Illustrates seven key skills of effective feedback.

'Coaching' (Video): Shows how to support managers in implementing coaching in an enthusiastic and effective way.

Melrose/Video Arts

'Coaching' (Video): Drama covering target setting following 'SMART' principle by tracing the progress of a management trainee trying to introduce targets in a Central Records Department.

Video Arts

'The Dreadful Appraisal' (Video/CD-ROM): How to review performance and set targets for the future in self-teach modules.

Index

Bold numbers indicate main entry.

acceptance of change   122, *see also*
    coping with change
achieving balance   43–4
administrative
    and service functions   63–6
    targets   88–9
assessment   13–15, 128, *see also under*
    review *and under* quantitative
'attraction to like'   110

balancing targets and responsibilities
    43, 93–7
behaviour   18, 21–3, 40–43, 52–3, 131,
    132–6
behavioural competencies/inputs   40–43
'best practice'   59
Boyatsis   60
building relationships   8
business
    process re-engineering   46
    structures   9

case studies   33–4, 43–5, 51–4, 55–7
Charles Handy   36–7
checklist
    for communications   104
    for effective targets   127
Coca Cola Italia   14, **51–4**
comfort zone   134–6
communication   83
    across functions   9
    checklist   104

skills   102–105
targets   88
company values   55–7
competency/ies   10, 35, 36, **38–43**
computing skills   89
confrontation   102, **109**
consistency   11, 24
consultants   14
continual review   97–8
continuous
    improvement   46–51
    training   10
coping with change   8, 9, 11, *see also*
    acceptance of change
core values of an organization   24
corporate
    environment, changes in the   7–9
    values   11
counselling   11
creativity   8, 42, 126
critical incident technique   52
culture and history of an organization
    1, 12
customer/supplier relationships   65, 67

decision making   8
departmental targets   125
desensitization   135, 136
development, bottom-up   82–3
developmental targets   80–81
diary technique   52
direction and motivation   11–12
distance learning   10

distinguishing targets from responsibilities   100

effort-to-results focus   21, 22
'emotional muscle'   52
empathy   102, 104, 105, 107
empowerment   27
entrepreneurship   8
example targets   87–90
'executive coach'   10
exercises (activities)   15, 57, 72, 86,
  111, 128, 139, 151–4

feedback   23, 26, 27, 102, **108–109**
  360 degree   14, 16, **51–4**, 55
finance, targets for   89
flexibility   9, 10, 42, 90
flooding   135, 136

group of similar job holders   95

'halo and horns effect'   110
Handy, Charles   36–7
Higgins and York   30–33
  case study   33–4
high achievers   136–9
human
  potential   131–9, 140
  resource function   14

imprinting onto subconscious mind
  146, 150–54
individual targets   125
'initiative approach'   46–7
In Search of Excellence   17–18
Institute of Personnel Management (and
  Development)   27, 28
integration with existing systems
  35–57
intellectual behaviours   52–3, see also
  behaviour
interpersonal skills   8, 52–3, **102–111**
interviews, management   52
joint problem solving   16, 21–3
judgemental behaviour   21–3, see also
  behaviour

key players, roles   14

leadership skills   62
'learning organization'   46
listening   102, 105–106

management   14
  -by-objectives schemes   21
  training   9
Management Charter Initiative   39
managerial targets   87, 125, 126
manager's role   12–15
managing internal change   151–4
measurement methods   82, 128
mentoring   10, 19
models for target setting   82
  training   117–21
multimedia   10
motivation   20

narrative-based approach   25–6
National Vocational Qualifications   39
NetTech   43
networking   8
numerical targets   79–80

objections to target setting   12–13,
  121–4
organizational
  competencies   40, 42
  messages   83–4
  targets   90, 125
outcomes   92–3
outputs   41–2

'paperless appraisal'   24
paperwork involved   23
perceptual distortions   110–11, 153
performance
  appraisal/management   **16–34**, 92–3
    history and trends   20–23
    pitfalls   30–33
  criteria questionnaire   52
personal development plans   53
personnel, targets for   89–90

persuasion and influence 8
Peters and Waterman 17–18
Peters, Tom 84
Power of Personal Influence 132
presentation(s) 135
  skills 88
'primacy and regency effect' 111
problem solving 8
  and decision making 48–9
processing information 8
promotion 69
psychometric analysis 11

quality circles 49–51
quantitative
  analysis 52
  targets 79–80
questioning 102, 106–108
questions during training 121–6

recruitment 38, 87
repertory grid 52
residential training course 118–21
results 22
review
  interpersonal skills and 102–111
  of target setting 91–101
  preparation for 92–3
  timescales 98–101
reward and remuneration systems
  36–8
routine jobs 126

selection of target areas 94
self
  -assertion statements 131, 136, 140,
    145–51
  -development 19
  -review 97–8
  -study 10
  -talk 133–6, 140–43, 151
seniority 61–3
senior management 14
skills training 9–11
staff management 87

stereotypes 110–11
'stretching' 11, 85, 127
success 9, 131, **137–9**, 140
  criteria **81–2**
  preparing the organization for
    58–73
  using targets to breed **84–6**
support 10, 11, 23
  ongoing 13, 48
  top-down 82–3

team
  briefing 88
  environments 72–3
  talk and vision building 143–5
  work 8, 9, 42
technical
  roles 67–8, 70–71
  skills 89
  targets 125
techniques of goal achievement
  140–54
tick-box approach 24
time
  constraints 59–61
  management 61, 87
timescales, from setting to review
  98–101
timing of pay review 37
total quality management (TQM)
  46–9, 90
training **9–11**
  and development needs/programmes
    19, 35, 38, **45–6**
  diversification 9
  example targets for 87
  managers and employees to set tar-
    gets **115–28**
two-way
  commitment 85–6, 127
  discussion 17, 23

understanding behaviour 132–6, *see
  also* behaviour
upward appraisal approach 26–7

videotapes   10
vision building   143–5
visualization   131, 137, 138, 140–43,
   146

weighting of targets   96–7, 125
what are targets?   78–9
workshops   115–18

Xilinx Semiconductor   55–7